# Napoleon Bonaparte
# and the
# Siege of Toulon

# Napoleon Bonaparte and the Siege of Toulon

The First Victory of a Future Emperor of France, 1793

Charles James Fox

LEONAUR

*Napoleon Bonaparte and the Siege of Toulon*
*The First Victory of a Future Emperor of France, 1793*
by Charles James Fox

First published under the title
*Napoleon Bonaparte and the Siege of Toulon*

Leonaur is an imprint
of Oakpast Ltd

ISBN: 978-0-85706-351-9 (hardcover)
ISBN: 978-0-85706-352-6 (softcover)

**http://www.leonaur.com**

# Contents

# Preface

The Siege of Toulon in 1793 is interesting and important, as a military event in the War of the First Coalition; as a political combination of the European Powers during the early part of the same war; and as a personal incident in the life of Napoleon Bonaparte. The following pages are the result of a study of the siege in which I have tried to give special attention to the second and third phases of the question. I have come to the conclusion that the political importance of the siege was considerable and that the English entered Toulon unexpectedly and intended to hold it simply as a pledge of indemnification; and secondly that the role of Bonaparte was very important and that he by directing the course of this siege, had here for the first time an influence upon the events of his time and consequently enters history.

As the last point has been much disputed and as the others have not yet been brought out, I have in attempting to demonstrate each, given as much as possible of the material used, together with frequent references, allowing him whom the subject may interest to draw his own conclusions, hoping however that they will coincide with those which in my opinion are the logical and just ones.

The first accounts of Napoleon's actions were written during, and under the influence of, the grandeur of the Consulate and First Empire. The part he played at Toulon was generally considered great and brilliant; but this prevalent opinion was based principally upon more or less inexact reminiscences of those who took part in the siege with him. Everybody accepted without going into particulars that the First Consul, or Emperor, began his career at Toulon, where his genius first attracted attention. At the *Restauration* royalists who had served at Toulon published accounts of the siege, which with regard to the role of Bonaparte, had rather the opposite tendency.

But as their principal aim was to bring forward their own actions and thereby win the favour of Louis XVIII, and as anti–Bonapartist statements needed then no foundation on fact, these writings are of no objective value. They reflect but the anti–Bonapartist and pro–English sentiment of the Court at this time. Thiers throws some light on Bonaparte's role at Toulon, attributing principally to him the fall of the city; but Thiers' Work was to vast to permit him to make any special study of the affair of Toulon. His account of it is filled with errors. The *Memoirs of Barras* (not published until 1895) furnish ample but quite untrustworthy material to those who wish to lessen the role of Bonaparte at this siege.

This same spirit of hostility to Napoleon prevails in Jung's *Bonaparte et son temps*. He too denies the importance of the role of Bonaparte at Toulon but he does not go much into particulars, nor did he study the question without prejudice. The eagerness with which he seeks an opportunity of defaming the name of Bonaparte is shown where he himself speaks of Napoleon (page 372 vol. 1) as an officer of 25 years when he wrote the *Souper de Beaucaire*, and then again deliberately accuses him (page 396) of giving a false age in stating that he was 25 after the siege of Toulon. Krebs and Morris in their work on *Campagnes in the Alpes* give a good general account of the siege, but the role of Bonaparte is passed by with the mere assertion that in the official records nothing is found to prove its importance.

It is true that in the documents of the Archives de la Guerre at Paris, no direct statement can be found that Napoleon Bonaparte took a very important part in the entire affair; but indirect proofs are by no means wanting, either here or in the English official reports. The two latest works on Toulon are those of Cottin and Chuquet. Cottin leaves the role of Bonaparte rather aside and using the English sources, writes on their action at Toulon. His work has the value of publishing important documents hitherto inaccessible in printed form; but with the same he has combined much doubtful detail derived from rather untrustworthy and contradictory sources.

His book has an anti–English tendency and fails to bring out the political importance of the affair of Toulon. Chuquet's work, an enlargement of two articles published in *Cosmopolis*, is of rather a popular character but it publishes for the first time some letters of Bonaparte and other important pieces. He goes into detail which is very difficult to control and the sources of which he has not always carefully considered. The role of Bonaparte is emphasized, but not in a manner convincing enough for a question so much in dispute.

In publishing this small volume I wish to take advantage of the opportunity to express my sincere gratitude to all my Professors at Heidelberg, and to mention my appreciation of the kindness of the late Professor Erdmannsdörffer and Professor Schäfer, whose generous aid and hospitality to foreigners I shall always try to emulate.

CONDITIONS UNDER WHICH TOULON SURRENDERED TO THE
ENGLISH AND SIEGE OF TOULON.

## CHAPTER 1

# France in 1793

In 1793 the French Revolution had advanced far in its impetuous course. In its commencement ill denned, its course hard to foresee, and uncertain, it had at its culmination formed itself into a definite, cruel and reckless system, the Terror. Power had passed from the right to the extreme left of the National Assembly, and there into hands which were capable of holding and using it. The execution of Louis XVI, the crowning act of the Revolution took place at the beginning of this year; shortly after followed the revolt in the Vendée: the first attempt at military rule was defeated as Dumouriez went over to the Austrians: the Girondists were overthrown by their more reckless and energetic rivals: then followed the uprising of two-thirds of the departments and of many large cities, Lyons, Marseilles, Toulon and Bordeaux.

The situation in the interior of France was very uncertain, and the dangers from without were great. After Neerwinden Belgium was lost and the Austrians advanced victoriously into Northern France. The Prussians retook Mayence and put an end to its revolutionary excesses. The Piedmontese forced their way over the Alps, the Spaniards came over the Pyrenees. The English were everywhere on the seas. It was under these conditions that France, or more strictly Revolutionary France, stood alone against the nations of Europe united in the pursuit of their different political ambitions, and in the hope of future advantages. For whatever may have been the origin of the Revolutionary Wars, the European nations, once united against France, were striving after their own interests, and these at the expense of France, who at this time seemed inevitably lost.

This however was not the case. Everyone knows the Peace of Campio Formio which followed that of Basel and others, yet it is by no means easy to explain clearly how the Republicans performed the seemingly impossible and forced upon the entire Continent such advantageous terms. The history of the Siege of Toulon gives an insight into these conditions, for one might almost say that here the War of the First Coalition took place on a smaller scale. The same forces stood opposing each other. On the one side, the European powers, England, Spain, Sardinia, Naples even Austria, as well as the French Royalists and *Emigres*; on the other the enthusiastic, almost fanatical, self-sacrificing, but uncertain Republican army, directed by a few ingenious leaders, among them Bonaparte and Victor, and supported at home by an active energetic government under the organizing genius of Carnot.

Everything was sacrificed to the object of the war. On the one side was discord, distrust, jealousy, and ill-directed egotism. The best energy of the European nations exhausted itself over the division of spoils which were still to be won. On the other side was geographic and political unity, together with a fanatical devotion to the one object. All passions, the ambition of the demagogue and of the soldier, even the fear of the Republicans, lead to the same end; namely, the liberating of France from the foreign invader. On the one hand it was a question of obtaining certain advantages, in the distribution of which lay the cause of future disagreement; on the other, it was a question of life and death; and this struggle for existence was carried on by energetic reckless men who had risen by their own force and ability, and who in the choice of their means were unhampered by any traditional, religious or even human considerations.

To understand a siege it is necessary, first to have an idea of the topographical and other military conditions of the place in which it is carried on. In the year 1793 Toulon, a city of some 28,000 inhabitants, was enclosed by a circle of fortifications which dated from the time of Vauban, but which had been continually improved and were now in fairly good condition. It was reputed one of the strongest fortifications in Europe. On the land side Toulon is surrounded by high mountains especially the massive ridge of Mount Faron on the north. From the city one road leads to Marseilles and another eastward toward Italy.

The Rivière Neuve flows from the north past the western side of the city, into the inner of the two harbours, which are called the Grande and Petite Rade. This river is dry in the summer. The fortifications on the north-west were Fort Pomets and the Redoute St. Andre (completed but not armed); on the north-east, Fort Rouge, Fort Blanc, and the intrenched camp, Ste. Anne. Mont Faron also protected the city on the north. On the east, to defend the road to Italy was Fort La Malgue. According to Napoleon, this fort was very carefully built. It protected also the Grande Rade. Fort Ste. Catherine and Fort L'Artigues, likewise on the east, were supported by Mont Faron.

On the west was Fort Malbousquet. It was merely a temporary fortification, but important through its position. Fort Missiessy was also on the west, on the north shore of the Petite Rade. The entrance to the Grande Rade was covered by Fort La Malgue, that of the Petite Rade by Fort Grosse Tour, on the eastern side, and by the coast batteries, Balaguier and Eguillette, on the western side. In general, more importance had been placed on the fortifications on the east of the city than on those on the west. It was supposed that all attacks were to come from the Italian side.

In Toulon, as in most of the cities and many of the departments, there was a revolutionary and a Royalist party, each striving to obtain power. In Toulon the Republicans found support in the Republican army under Carteaux. The Royalists, in accordance with their policy at that time, sought help from outside.[1] The English squadron had been seen for weeks before Toulon, where her Admiral, Lord Hood, stood watching the large French fleet in the harbour. To destroy this formed part of his plan; which was to win and hold for England the supremacy of the Mediterranean. The Royalists of Marseilles and Toulon were in constant communication, and were secretly forming plans.

A certain undecided portion of the population was to be won over to their side. For some time they cherished the plan of inviting the English to enter. In some manner the English representative in Turin, John Trevor, who was well informed on the affairs of Italy and the Mediterranean, got news of this intention and wrote as early as July 21 to Hood, informing him of the possibility of an appeal for help from the people of Toulon. Hood seemed, however, to have given the matter but little attention. His object was still the French fleet. A few days before, on July 19, he had sent a Lieutenant Cook into Toulon to negotiate an exchange of prisoners; permitting him to wait twenty-four hours for a reply.

Cook returned bringing with him a list of the French ships in Toulon, and other useful information. It is possible, although all evidence is wanting, that Cook, who was Hood's nephew, entered even at this

---

1. de Brécy. "*Un sentiment presque unaninie inspira le projet d'envoyer un parlementaire au commandant anglais pour lui demander son concours et son assistance.*"

time, into communication with the Royalists. The Royalists resorted to a trick to win over the still undecided portion of the inhabitants. The fear of a bread famine was held out before the people; although there were provisions for three months at hand. Thaon de Revel, the commander of the Piedmontese troops wrote: "*L'appréhension de la famine fut la consideration qui décida les habitans. Les chefs avaient persuadé a la multitude que bientôt elle manquerait de pain si l' on ne traitait avec les Anglais; quoique dans le fait il y eut du grain pour plus de trois rnois.*" [2]

Nelson, who at the time of the siege, was sailing in and out of the harbour of Toulon, wrote "Famine had done what force could not have done." [3] In this manner the people were deceived and won over. Negotiations with Hood commenced first from Marseille, then from Toulon, the latter being of much more interest to the English.

At first one spoke of an importation of grain into Marseille, finally of the conditional surrender of Toulon to the English. After holding a Council of War Hood gave out, on August 23, a preliminary declaration, which was soon followed by a proclamation. Both were sent to Marseille and Toulon. The declaration said: That if the people of Toulon and Marseille declare openly for monarchy; if the vessels are disarmed and the harbour and forts put provisionally in Hood's charge, the people of Provence may count upon the assistance of the British fleet: the rights of property and of the individual shall be protected: further, that Hood's only object is the restoration of peace and that then all will be returned "*conformément à l'inventaire qui en sera fait*".

In the Proclamation Hood gives a "*tableau fièdle*" of the "*malheureuse condition*" of the French nation during the last four years, and declares that the European nations see no remedy to such evils other than reestablishment of monarchy in France. He offers his protection and aid to establish "*un gouvernment regulier et de maintainer la paix et la tranquillité dans l'Europe.*" Hood's proclamation arrived too late in Marseilles; the approaching Republican army made it impossible to continue the negotiations. In Toulon the most stormy debates took place in the Sections when Lieutenant Cook announced Hood's offer. The Royalists carried off the victory, in spite of all opposition of the other party, and of the hostile attitude of the French ships in the harbour. The Sections decided for the entrance of the English, but under several conditions.

Among others; the present constitution was to be replaced by the

---

2. *Memoirs.*
3. Letters Sept. 14th. *Nelson dispatches.*

monarchical government, under the Constitution of 1791; [4] civil and military officers were to retain their places. The provisioning of the city was to be assured; an inventory was to be made of the vessels and of all material in the port.

These conditions were carried back by Cook to Hood, who accepted them. His present fleet was however not strong enough to risk entering alone. He therefore asked assistance from the Spanish Admiral Langara who at first refused, but consented on a second invitation from Hood, who accompanied this invitation with a copy of his intended proclamation. In the meantime Hood published his second proclamation to the inhabitants of Toulon. It was dated August 28th and declared: as the Sections of Toulon have declared Louis XVII as their legitimate sovereign and for monarchy according to the constitution of 1791, he takes possession of Toulon and will guard it *"en dépôt pour Louis XVII jusqu' au rétablissement de la paix en France"*.

The next day as the Spanish fleet appeared in sight Hood sailed into the harbour, the Spanish following. [5] The seamen of the French fleet were divided into two parties, the Jacobins and the Royalists. The first showed in the beginning a determination to oppose the landing of the English, but were held in check by the Royalists and the land batteries. Finally, threatened by the English and Spanish, they found it better to take advantage of a chance to escape, than to offer resistance. The crew of seven ships succeeded in getting away. Hood and Langara received a most enthusiastic reception from the inhabitants and officials of Toulon. An excellent understanding existed between the two admirals. A thousand marines and about 300 sailors from each fleet were landed immediately at Fort LaMalgue. [6]

On September 12th the news of the fall of Toulon reached London by way of Turin. It caused in government circles quite as much surprise as satisfaction. It was decided to collect troops and send them to Hood without deranging the plans of campaign in general. The first intention was to send 5000 British troops, raised in Ireland, and 5000 Hessians. [7] As early as September 14th, and at Pitt's suggestion, [8]

4. This constitution was always referred to, and is spoken of in the following pages, as the constitution of 1789.

5. *Journal of Samuel Lord Hood*. Admiralty Records. Public Record Office.

6. Letter from Graham to Sir William Hamilton. *Correspondence*. British Museum. Manuscript Department. Egerton 2638.

7. Letter Dundas to Sir James Murray. Sept. 14. War Office. *British Army on Continent.* 1793. Record Office.

8. Letter Pitt to Grenville. Sept 7. *Manuscripts of J. B. Fortescue.*

instructions were sent to Sir Morton Eden, the English ambassador at Vienna to ask for Austrian troops. These were promised, but never arrived. More about the negotiations concerning the will be given later.

Here it might be well to insert an account of the political situation of Europe at this time. Three important questions preoccupied more or less, the different cabinets. The war against the Republic, affairs in Poland and Austria's resumed plan of exchanging the Netherlands for Bavaria. Nearly all the nations were joined in the struggle with France but the attention of several of them Austria, Prussia, Russia, an others was much diverted by the other two questions. The news of the second division of Poland brought Thugut, whose anti-Prussian policy was well known, into power in Vienna. An understanding between Austria and England was the result. This power, (England) as well as the other European nations, now taking for granted, (and under existing conditions it was almost pardonable) that France would fall, directed its best thoughts and energy to her future dismemberment, arid to its share of the "Indemnification." The plans of the English government, having taken rather a definite form, full instructions were sent to Eden in Vienna.

They were dated Whitehall. Sept. 7. [9] and contained, first, an account of Austria's plans, as they have been stated in England, namely:

> . . . the making permanent acquisitions, to as large an extent as they are practicable, in the Low Countries, in Alsace and Loraine, and in the intermediate parts of the frontier of France. No similar communication has as yet been made on the part of His Majesty, but the circumstances and situation of affairs have made it sufficiently evident that whatever indemnification is to be acquired by this country must be looked for in the foreign settlements and colonies of France. In these objects the interest of the two Courts are so far from clashing that His Majesty has an interest in seeing the House of Austria strengthen itself by acquisition on the French frontier, and the very circumstance of that interest should make the Emperor see with pleasure the relative increase of the naval and commercial resources of this country beyond those of France As to the Powers who are already engaged in the war it does not appear that much can be done by Austria, at least in the present moment towards securing the co-operation of Spain. But no endeavours will be

9. Foreign Office. Austria. Sir Morton Eden. Aug. to Oct. 93. Public Record Office.

omitted by His Majesty for that purpose...

In speaking of the coolness between Austria and Sardinia:

.....the idea once entertained by the Court of Vienna of ex-ending the frontier of the Milanese at the expense of the King of Sardinia is, I trust, abandoned, but if brought forward again, must be strongly discouraged by you....

As regards Prussia:

....it is obvious that the interest of the Emperor is as much concerned as that of His Majesty in securing even at the ex-pense of some sacrifice the co-operation and assistance of the King of Prussia. If no step is taken to remove the increasing jealousy between those two courts the worst consequences may be expected from them.

Then follows advice to Austria to renounce her claim on Bavaria in order to avoid Prussia's jealousy. The Elector might then take an active part in the war, might send troops to His Majesty

.... who would not be unwilling to incur a considerable ex-pense for an object of so much importance to the common cause.....

As to Russia,

His Majesty's endeavours to obtain the active co-operation of that power have proved ineffective. The assistance of a body of troops having ultimately been refused to His Majesty except on terms which, independent of other objections, would have committed this country with respect to the interior of France beyond what His Majesty judged to be advisable or prudent.

.... In the Mediterranean the interests of this country are, that our naval superiority over France should be maintained and there is no reason to doubt of this point being sufficiently secured....

Here Grenville mentions the necessity of the assistance of 12,000 or 15,000 Austrian troops for affairs in the Mediterranean:

.... I have mentioned to you His Majesty's disposition to con-nect himself by a defensive alliance with the Emperor, and I have stated that you are at liberty to give the strongest assur-ances on this head. The basis of such an alliance would naturally be, as I have explained to Count Starhenberg the same with of the ancient system by which the two countries were formally united: the securing a barrier against France, the retaining the Netherlands under the lawful sovereignty of Austria, the securing and augmentation of the commerce of the Maritime Powers, and the Mutual guaranty of all possessions antecedent to the war.

The foregoing instructions give an insight into political relations at this moment. The following extract from a letter to Grenville, from Lord St. Helens, the English Ambassador at Madrid, completes it to some extent.[10] It was dated Madrid, August 28.

.... I understand that the Duke of Alcudia has testified a great deal of Pique and Dissatisfaction to the Prussian and Austrian Ministers on account of the late capitulations of Mentz and Valanciennes concerning that from the vague and indefinite terms they were drawn the French government will consider themselves as at liberty to employ these garrisons in their armies on this Frontier. There appears great reason to hope that these alarms may prove groundless. However this seeming want of attention to the interests of this crown on the part of the Emperor and the King of Prussia has increased the sentiments of jealousy against those sovereigns, which have been so long entertained here, and which I observe to be studiously kept up and inflamed by the agents of the French Princes.

With regard to England, the Spanish Minister's language is still friendly and cordial, however, I am told that some ill-intentioned Persons have been endeavouring to persuade him that we have acted uncandidly by this Court in concluding a Treaty with Naples without their knowledge, and I therefore take the liberty of submitting to your Lordship whether if that Treaty contained nothing of a secret nature it might not be advisable to communicate it here without loss of time. . . . .

Here is the political situation in a few words. England looked for indemnification outside of Europe; an increase of her commerce and supremacy over France in the Mediterranean. Her object was to bring the war to a fortunate termination and for that reason to hold the European nations together. She was willing to make financial sacrifices for the common cause. She would not commit herself as to the future government in France. Austria wished to increase her possessions in

---

10. Foreign Office. Spain. Lord St. Helens and Consuls' dispatches Aug. to Dec. 1793. Public Record Office.

the Netherlands and in Alsace; she was jealous of Prussia. She hoped also to extend her Milanese territory, and there was jealousy between her and Sardinia. She was not quite so decided about continuing her plan of obtaining Bavaria. Spain had cause of ill-will against Austria and Prussia. Russia continued her policy of refraining from any active part in the war against France. England had signed treaties with Sardinia,[11] Naples, Hesse and Baden, by which they agreed to furnish her troops. Prussia's attention was turned toward Poland and she was already wavering in her policy of war against the Republic.

The English government was not quite satisfied with Lord Hood's declaration. Grenville wrote to Eden Sept. 14.[12]

> Lord Hood has been induced by circumstances and by the great advantage which was in view, to go further with respect to the Interior state of France and to the Futur Government to be established there, than was in contemplation according to the ideas stated to you in my late dispatch. You will explain the circumstances to the Austrian Minister and you will add that on this account as well as from the change which the event of Toulon produced in our situation it may perhaps be advisable that some public measure should be taken on this subject by this court, and that of Vienna jointly. The ideas on this subject which are entertained by His Majesty's Ministers will be transmitted to you with as little delay as possible.

In Spain the news of Toulon's surrender was well received. St. Helens wrote to Grenville, Sep 6.[13]

> I need not say that this court are highly satisfied with these advices, and above all with Lord Hood's invitation to Admiral Langara to partake in his success, and that they profess the utmost readiness to co-operate with us cordially in every step of the business.

The news of Hood's entrance was also welcomed by the Royalists and Emigrants, and for a time it was supposed that other cities would follow the example of Toulon.

---

11. Letter Dundas to O'Hara. 18th Dec. Letters from Secry. Dundas to Lieut. Gen. Dundas. 1793-94. British Museum. Mss. Dept. Additional 27,594.
"By treaty 26. April. Sardinian Majesty in consequence of payment of subsidy has bound himself to furnish his majesty 20,000 troops free of any further expense."
12. Public Record Office.
13. St. Helens. Public Record Office.

In the information sent to the Foreign Office; dated Sept 20.[14] one reads

*On croit que les Royalistes à Brest dont il y a grand norabre feront en sorte que la flotte renterra sous peu de jours et qu'on y proclamera comme a Toulon Louis 17*

De Saint Croix, one of the Emigrants in London, wrote to Grenville, dated London, Sept. 15.[14]

*Lorsque j'eus avant bier l'honneur d'écrire a Votre Excellence je ne connaissais point les deux proclamations de M. L'Amiral Hood. Permettez-moi mi-lord de vous en exprimer et comme français et comme individu toute ma reconnaissance. Puissent tons les cabinets adopter ce language: il y a plus de gloire à parler ainsi qu'à vaincre. . . . Vous nous rendez Mylord quelque confience et quelque sécurité: vous commandez l'estime de l'Europe et vous lui donnez un grand exemple.*

The opinion in England was somewhat divided as to the advisability of retaining Toulon, even temporarily, but all were united in rejoicing that the French fleet was in English hands. It was even suggested that upon a good opportunity it might be burned and the town given up. As the siege went on it was not hard to see that the question of what was to be done with the French fleet became a most delicate one. It was partly upon this point that the difference arose between the English and Spanish Admirals, and later their respective Governments. Lord Sheffield wrote September 15th to Auckland [15]

I see no use of encumbering ourselves with Toulon unless we carry home the French fleet. I should certainly have taken advantage of the kind of resistance made by the French fleet, by hauling into the inner road and would have burnt them all to save further embarrassment.

Pitt speaks of the taking of Toulon as a "most fortunate event." [16]
The Marquis of Buckingham wrote to Grenville[17] Sept 15.

We have only to pray that the patriots may besiege Toulon and that the issue of the contest may be the conflagration of the docks and fleet.

And on Sept 29th.

You must be prepared to meet much opposition to the idea of

---

14. Foreign Office. Domestic Papers. March to Dec. 1793. Public Record Office.
15. Auckland Papers. British Museum. Mss. Vol. 12. Additional 34,452.
16, 17. Letter to Grenville. Sept 7, 15, 29, Oct. 4 Manuscripts of Fortescue.

indemnification which the emigrants now in London are loud in reprobating. At the same time the people of Brest and Toulon cannot be very anxious for the slices which may be required from France on the side of the Pays Bas and of Lorain, or even of Piedmont; and whether they are or no it is good to habituate people early to the sound of such a proposition

On Oct. 4th.

I conclude that our fleet winters at Toulon and refits with French stores taken upon a valuation; but at all events, I hope that you will retain the superiority in those seas even over the Spaniards, whose operations except those of Langara do not please me.

Nelson wrote Oct. 7th.

Whether we shall be able to maintain our most extraordinary acquisition time only can determine, however one hour will burn the French fleet [18] . . . .

The plan of D'Alcudia, the Spanish minister was[19] that the combined squadrons should seize the first opportunity of forcibly removing all the Toulon ships to some place of greater security, as Port Mahon or Carthagena.

When the *Comité du Salut Public* heard of the surrender of Toulon they sent off the following laconic note to the "*Representants du Peuple*" with the Republican army at Toulon.

*Citoyens collègues . . Nous avons appris avec indignation la perfide trahison de Toulon dont vous nous informez par votre dépêche du 29 (sic) Août: du courage, de la fermeté de la constance: nous vaincrons les royalists, les despots et les traitres.* [20]

---

18. *Nelson Dispatches.*
19. St. Helens, to Grenville Oct. 2. Record Office.
20. *Reponse du Comité.* Aug. 28. *Re cueil Aulard.*

# Arrival of Bonaparte

Carteaux, the Republican General, entered Marseilles on August 25.[1] He did not march directly on Toulon as he was waiting for reinforcements from the army of Italy, which were approaching from the east, nor did he dare leave Marseilles unprotected. Toulon was threatened from the east and west by two armies, just as the allies arrived. The English especially were ill prepared in a military way, having no soldier of a higher rank than captain.[2] It was impossible to do much towards fortifying the town, which, especially on the western side, where the French had never expected an attack, was rather exposed.

One feared somewhat a *coup de main* by Carteaux, aided by the discontented in the town, of which there were a large number. From the beginning the Republicans were not idle. "*Nous avons donné l'ordre de faire sonner le tocsin dans toutes les communes du départment du Var et de faire marcher tous les citoyens depuis l'âge de 16 ans jusqu'à 60*". This shows a praiseworthy activity, but to allow such crowds to be hurled by incompetent generals against a fortified city was worse than foolish.

Carteaux's advance guard occupied the passes of Ollioules on the 29th of August. The English and Spanish hearing of it, promptly drove the Republicans back. This was the first action and there were but a few casualties. This position however, was important, as it commanded the road to Marseilles, and also the communications with La Seyne, a village on the south-west corner of the Petite Rade; but it was too far from Toulon for the Allies to hold it in their present condition. Carteaux who had just (Sept 4.) been appointed to the command of the besieging army,[3] which was to be independent of the army of Italy,

1. *Lettre de Salicetti.* Aug 25. R. A.
2. Letter. T. Graham to Sir William Hamilton. British Museum. Mss. Egerton. 2638.
3. *Armée du Siege de Toulon. Archives de la guerre.*

made preparations to retake it.

On September 7 the attack took place and was successful. [4] The Allies retreated to the town with a small loss: the Republicans lost but one man, and Dommartin, who commanded the artillery was severely wounded. This slight success of the Republicans caused a somewhat bad impression in the town. The Republicans now closed in from the east and west. Carteaux, who commanded the western division in person, established his headquarters at Ollioules and extended his position from Faubrégas to Baon-de-Quatres-Heures. Lopoype, who had come from the Italian Army, commanded on the east. His headquarters were at Solliès-Farlède. Lapòype was an ex-marquis whose Jacobinisme was much less to questioned than his ability as a general. He was not much inferior to Carteaux however, especially in this kind of military work. His wife was a prisoner in Toulon and this fact hampered him in his movements. [5]

The Republicans were very weak in artillery, and some of it had to be left in Marseille *"pour foudroyer cette ville s'il s'y manifestait quelque mouvement."* Now they were even deprived of their chief of artillery, Donmartin. With the material at hand however, Carteaux had erected a battery on the west side, to burn the fleet: but its position, far out of range of either the fleet or town, was laughable. [6] Reinforcements continued to arrive on each side and both parties prepared themselves for the struggle. Spain was especially prompt in sending reinforcements. [7] By returns taken on Sep 12. [8] there were over 5000 troops and sailors on shore: of these 3400 were Spanish and about 1600 English. This force quite exceeded that of Carteaux in efficiency and probably in numbers. Hood wrote on Sept 14 the "Enemy not yet provided with artillery."

The hopes of the Allies might well rise, for who could have suspected, unless it was the young Corsican himself, and at this very moment the besieging army had received a most formidable reinforcement?

On September 16 or 17 (*see note following*), the direction of the

---

4. *Lettre de Carteaux à Lapòype.* Sept 8. *Archives de la guerre. Lettre* Capt. Cook to Gen. Ed. Smith. Sept 7. Barrow's *Life of Sidney Smith.*
5. *Lapòype à Bouchotte.* Sept 11. *Archives de la Guerre.*
6. *Carteaux à Lopoype.* Sept 8.
7. Letters from St. Helens. Sept 18. Record Office
8. Letter from St. Helens. Sept 25. R. O.
    Graham to Hamilton. Sept 14.
        Correspondence. British Museum. Mss. Egerton.  2638.

principal arm of Carteaux's army was put under the control of Napoleon Bonaparte, then 24 years of age, and a captain of Artillery. A new period in Napoleon's life began here. In after years when he was preoccupied about his own history, he wished that it should begin with the siege of Toulon. This is seen especially in his *Memoirs* from St. Helena. It is usually said that in so doing his object was to pass over the preceding period in Corsica, which would not tend to make him popular in France.

This may no doubt be partially true, but it is none the less so that these three months, before the walls of Toulon, were three of the most important in his life. Here his entire career was changed. Others besides himself were convinced of his ability, even of his genius. He was thrown into close contact with the French people; and became at last one of them. His ambition was freed from the little island of Corsica, and bound itself to the destinies of the French nation; soon afterwards to control them.

★★★★★★★

Note:—The exact date when Napoleon arrived in Toulon is difficult to place. He says in his *Memoires* the 12th. of Sept. Chuquet believes he has proved that he arrived on the 16th. of Sept. (Page 171 note) "*On ignorait jusqu'ici le jour où Bonaparte arriva devant Toulon. Ses memoires disent tantôt le 12 Sept. tantôt douze à quinze jours après la prise d'Ollioules, du 19 au 22 Septembre. Mais il est sûrement le 15 à Marseille* (cf. pièce LXIX; a letter from Marseille, dated Sept 15) *et, suivant une lettre de Salicetti, il fait le 17 à Ollioules les préparatifs d'une attaque; il est donc arrivé le 16 au quartier général du Beausset. N'ecrit-il pas d'ailleurs pendant les siège 'les batteries furent établies trois jours après son arriveé?' Or la batterie de la Montagne date du 19 Septembre.*"

In the first place the contradiction in Napoleon's *Memoirs* can be explained. There are accounts of Toulon in two volumes written by different generals. According to the First volume Napoleon arrived 12 or 15 days after the taking of Ollioules, which according to this volume took place on Sept 10 The arrival of Bonaparte would therefore have taken place between the 22nd and 25th of Sept, and not the 19th and 22nd as Chuquet puts it. This volume was corrected by Napoleon, but he probably gave no great attention to such details. The third volume was dictated by Napoleon and contains a twice as lengthy account of Toulon. Here he says expressly that he arrived on the 12th of Sept.

As to the date of the battery L,a Montagne, Chuquet gives it (page 172) as Sept. 9, then (page 179) as Sept 12, and finally (page 206) Sep. 18. The evening of the 17th is the proper date, as on the morning of the 18th the battery fires on the ships. (Hood's *Journal*) On the 16th Dommartin was still, at least nominally, head of the artillery (*Carteaux à Lapòype, Archives de la Guerre*) and on the 17th Napoleon directs it. (*Lettre Salicetti* Sept 26. R. A.) Salicetti writes *"nous arrêtâmes le citoyen Buonaparte et nous lue ordonnâmes de remplacer Dommartin"*

It is quite possible that Napoleon was employed for a few days about Toulon before he received Dommartin's position. He must have first proved his ability to the *Representants*; or have influenced them in some way (he knew Salicetti) before receiving the position which should otherwise have fallen to Lieut-colonel Sugney, who commanded the artillery under Lapòype. It is a significant fact that on Sept 16, Carteaux writes to Lapòype, *"c'est l'artillerie qui fait toute la besogne"*, as if it were a fact of which he has just become convinced: also in direct contradiction to his previous ideas.

Napoleon may have arrived on the 12th and yet have returned to Marseilles on the 15th. If he did not arrive until the 16th then his statement that he found almost no artillery, is incorrect, because just at this time some artillery at least begins to arrive. ( Carteaux à Lapòype, Sept 16. A. G.) Napoleon probably forwarded it himself from Marseille where he was employed at the arsenal. By the September 19 Carteaux is aiding him as he writes to Bonaparte (Letter, A. G. ) *"Je viens de recevoir votre lettre et je vais envoyer à la Municipalite pour vous procurer tous les objets que vous me demandez"*.

★★★★★★

At the end of these three months he was no longer a neglected captain but a young general with a career behind him, as well as a far greater and more definite one before him. He had had an insight into the world of that day, and understood the political situation of his time. The means by which he was to satisfy his ambition were no longer vague dreams of the imagination but definite and deep-laid plans founded on an experience of men and a knowledge of conditions. His actions in Corsica must have now appeared to him as youthful. Feeling that he had matured in these three months it was no wonder that he should have believed that his career commenced at Toulon.

When Napoleon arrived he found the army in a most pitiable state; very little artillery [9] and what there was placed in a position harmless to the enemy;[10] the generals without a plan, or rather with a new one each day, but most of them useless. [11] The staff did not even have a map of the town and surrounding country. [12] Napoleon saw what any other instructed officer would have seen, that the first object was to attack the fleet in the harbour, and soon selected the best position for doing so. He set to work immediately but before long he had a misunderstanding with Carteaux, who knew little about artillery. However, Bonaparte had very wisely assured himself of the all-powerful *Representants du Peuple*; with one of these, Salicetti, a Corsican, he had been in personal connection before. In fact, in September Salicetti had caused Napoleon's brother Joseph to be appointed *Commissaire de Guerre* with the rank of Lieutenant-Colonel.

These *Representants du Peuple* were characteristic of this period of the Revolution. Sent out to the armies and into the cities by the Central Government, their duty was to watch the generals, spur them on, and excite the patriotism of the people; also to send frequent information to the Government in Paris. They were all powerful, and at the same time quite independent. All mistakes were attributed to the generals, for whom the guillotine was not an unusual penalty; the *representants* simply appointed new ones in their places. They incorporated the idea of the absolute supremacy of the civil power over military and all other. No other instances of a similar character are found in history. Salicetti, Barras, Gasparin, Albitte and others were at Toulon; Salicetti during the entire siege.

Little they suspected that the young artillery officer, who courted their favour, flattered their pride, and won their confidence, would in a few years change the face of things, overturn the despotism of the demagogue, and erect in its place a quite as despotic military power

---

9. Letter from Barras, 6 Sept. R.A. and from Lapòype to Carteaux Sept. 14, A. G.
10. Letter from Albitte 9 Sept. R.A.
11. Letter from Lapòype to Bouchotte, 11 Sept. A. G., letter from Carteaux to Lapòype 14 Sept. A. G. And letter from Carteaux to Mtre. de la Guerre—15 Sept. A. G.
12. *Carteaux au Ministere de la Guerre*, Sept 12 and Sept 15. A. G.

but less unjust, creative and lawgiving. The beginning of this transition was seen in the Italian campaign of 1796-97, when General Clark sent out to watch the young General Bonaparte, decided to cast in his lot with Napoleon rather than with the Directory. Napoleon got an excellent insight into the ways of these representatives at Toulon, which no doubt aided him much in winning over Clark.

On September 17[13] Napoleon erected his first battery. The next day it began to take effect, and the first serious attack commenced. On the 18th and 19th the ships of the Allies and this battery had a tremendous engagement. [14] On the 20th, the second battery was erected and "fired with more effect on the ships"; "Gunboats suffered considerably and the St. George had 21 men killed and wounded by the bursting of one of her lower deck guns, the land batteries were silenced before two o'clock, but altogether we had lost about 70 men wounded or killed. Lord Hood became anxious about the shipping and that evening it was determined to occupy the Heights of Grasse." [15]

On September 20 the following was inserted in Lord Hood's *journal*. "The floating battery No. 1 hauled off, having received much damage." This is the official record of Napoleon's first hostile act against the British. On September 21st "Cannonade still in the northwest arm". "Mr. Gourly and people returned from the Floating battery No. 3, it being sunk by the enemy's shot in the N. W. Arm".

Napoleon's first batteries had been firing but a day or so when the possibility of being forced to leave the harbour was brought forcibly home to the two Admirals. The question immediately arose what was, in such a case, to be done with the French fleet. From now on this question remained a source of contention between the Admirals, and also between their respective courts. This difference had disastrous results and Napoleon's cleverly placed batteries were the cause of it. It was his first act that had any influence upon the events of his time, and it took place within the first few days of his arrival before Toulon. On October 3rd the Duke of Alcudia wrote to St. Helens:

> As the case though remote may possibly occur in which the Spanish and English squadrons may be obliged to abandon the anchorage of Toulon from there being so much molested by bombs and red hot shells, as not to be able to remain there, His Majesty's pleasure upon this point has been signified to Admiral

---

13. *Lettre Salicetti*, Sept. 26. R. A., Letter *Mulgrave-Gazette*.
14. *Hood's journal*, September 18th.
15. Letter from Thomas Graham, September 25th. *Life of Graham*.

Langara by the Minister of Marine on the 1st instant, leaving, however, to the prudent discretion of the admiral, to settle and resolve in concert with Lord Hood whatever may according to existing circumstances, be found most advisable. [16]

This is an official record of Napoleon's work during the first few days at Toulon. In the same letter the Spanish Minister proposed that in case it became necessary to leave the port, "Admiral Langara shall sail, with all French ships that can be put to sea to the islands of Hieres, or whatever other place he may appoint in concert with Lord Hood, as most convenient, carrying in them all the artillery, ammunition, arms and stores which they can bring; leaving a manifest or protest to the government of Toulon, if the latter should not abandon the place that all ships of the French navy shall be kept and taken care of, to be delivered, at a proper opportunity, to their lawful sovereign".

"This instruction" writes St. Helens "was prepared in consequence of the information that had been received from thence stating that the enemy had succeeded in establishing a battery which in some sort commanded the harbours and roads". [17]

It will be seen that the "manifest or protest" referred to by Alcudia was apparently all that was to be left to the people of Toulon who had confided themselves to the English and Spaniards. Alcudia further proposed that such ships as could not be removed should be sunk or set on fire. As this was later on actually done, it will be seen bow the Spanish regarded their own proposal, (see part 2). I do not mean to imply in the least that the English were any more sincere in their dealings with the people of Toulon or that they had any more scruples in disposing of the French fleet. Hood wrote to London that he used the French ships against the batteries thinking it better that they should be sunk than his own. [18]

To prevent the enemy's batteries from being placed in a still more dangerous position, on the Heights of Grasse, Admiral Gravina and Lord Mulgrave, the English commander landed at midnight Sept. 21st with about 500 men at Balaguier, and gained the wooded heights above without seeing any of the enemy. A post was established before daybreak on the most commanding point: in the afternoon it was attacked by 600 men who approached under cover of the wood. They were repulsed. The next day more troops were sent out, woods were

---

16. St. Helens. R. O. Published by Cottin.
17. St. Helens to Grenville. Oct. 9th. R. O.
18. Hood to Philip Stephens. Oct. 7. Admirals dispatches Mediterranean 1793. R. O.

cut down in abatis, and the post was well supplied with cannon. There were now 800 men on the spot.

Here the Allies gained a most decided advantage; they had seized and fortified the most vulnerable point surrounding Toulon, and the harbour. Napoleon on his arrival had recognized the importance of this position and went to Carteaux *"pour lui offrir de le faire entrer dans Toulon avant huit jours, s'il voulait faire occuper en force la position du Caire* (the Heights of Grasse) *de manière que l'artillerie put sur-le-champ placer des batteries a l'extremité des caps de l'Eguillette et de Balaguier"*.[19] Carteaux whose favourite tactics were the use of the *arme blanc* failed to see the importance of this position and allowed the allies to proceed him. [20] Finally when he did make the attack, it was done in such a half-spirited manner as to be easily repulsed.

Napoleon took no part in this attack, but on the very same day his battery sunk one of the floating batteries of the enemy. He as well as the *Representants du Peuple* were loud in accusing Carteaux and lamenting his failure to take the position.

> *Pourquoi ne l'avons-nous pas fait? Parceque le général que nous avi-ons cru comprendre et adopter notre plan n'y avait aucune confiance quoique celui que vous aviez envoyé de Paris fût exactement le même: parce ceux qui l'entourent sont encore plus ignorants et plus entêtés que lui: parceque ni les uns, ni les autres n'ont aucune connaissance ni des hommes qu'ils mènent ni des machines militaires, ni de leurs effets: parce que toute l'armée n'ayant trouvé jusqu'à présent aucune résist-ance dans son expédition est toute decouragée de celle que lui presente Toulon*—*si l'absence de Carteaux* (it was supposed that he was going to the Army of Italy) *nous donne un général et des officiers supérieurs qui sentent mieux l'importance de la point des Vallons nous tenterons encore d'en chasser les Anglais.*[21]

Napoleon wrote on Nov. 14th to the Minister of War, referring to this attack: [22]

> *Dans ce moment là* (while his batteries were fighting the enemy's ships) *les ennemis comprenant l'insuffisance de leur artillerie navale risquèrent le tout pour le tout et débarquèrent a l'Eguillette; ils us-*

19. *Memoires de Napoléon.*
20. Attack on Hauteurs de Grasse. Hood's *Journal.* Letter of Mulgrave in *Gazette.* Letter from Graham, *Life of Graham. Memoires and Correspondence of Napoleon.* Sali-cetti to Comité Sept. 26 R. A.
21. *Lettre de Salicetti,* Sept. 26th. R. A.
22. *Correspondance de Napoléon.*

*sent dû être écrasé dans leur descent; la fatalité ou notre ineptie voulut qu'elle leur réêssit. Peu de jours après ils y eurent des pièces de 24, un chemin convert et des palissades, quelques jours après, des secours considérables leur arrivèrent de Naples et d'Espagne. Je compris que l'affaire de Toulon était manquée et qu'il fallait se resoudre à un siege.*

From here up to the first of October nothing of great importance happened. The fleet and land batteries continued an artillery duel; reinforcements arrived gradually for each side. Part of the French squadron was put in commission under the French Admiral Trogoff. Toulon was declared a free port and well supplied with provisions, chiefly from Spain and the Spanish islands. On Sept 23 the Republicans heard the fire of 21 guns from each ship of the fleet. It was in honour of the coronation of Louis XVII. [23]

On Oct. 1 Carteaux received the following note.

"*Les troupes de la Republique viennent d'enlever la montague du Faron, ses retranchements et sa redoute. Signé La Poype*". [24]

The commanding position of Faron was of great importance and La Poype decided to attack it. From the northern side it was considered inaccessible, except at Pas de la Masque, where one might reach the top by a narrow zigzag path; the English considered a strong post of sixty men sufficient to hold this pass. On the night of Sept. 30 La Poype formed his three attacking columns. The one on the right was to ascend the northwest end; it was under the command of Victor. La Poype commanded the centre column, which was to attack at Pas de la Masque; the column on the left was to make a false attack. Victor led his column up the hill, along the ridge of the mountain eastward to Pas de la Masque; he drove the picket back into the *redoute* of Faron, assailed this on all sides at once, and cleared it out just as the enemy had run up their signal for help.

While La Poypes triumphant note was on its way to Carteaux the alarming news of the taking of Faron reached the town. Reinforcements, of the best troops and in large numbers, as well as field pieces should have been hurried to Victor and his men. But this was not done. A few men did arrive before the end of the day, but they were such as did more harm than good. The ridge of Faron is formed by several heights running east and west. A deep ravine running northward from Toulon cuts deep into Mount Faron perpendicularly; it

---

23. Hood's *Journal*.
24. *Lettre de Salicetti*. Oct. 1. R. O.

runs almost through to the northern side leaving only a narrow ridge connecting the heights on the east and west of this valley, which is called Valbourdin. On the south-western side of the ascent was Fort St. Antoine and on the south-eastern Fort Faron.

The Allies, in contrast to the Republicans, showed the greatest activity and determination. At 7 o'clock the news reached the town: a council of war was held and the immediate attack determined upon. At 8 o'clock the troops started. English, Spanish Piedmontese and Neapolitans, good troops and of four nationalities, started forward to attack Victor and his small force. The result would not have been at all certain, had Victor been able to rely upon his troops; they were new, of inferior quality and such as are easily panic-stricken. Lord Mulgrave and Colonel de Revel lead the English and Piedmontese column up the south-west side of the mountain.

On the most western ridge they met about 200 of the enemy, whom they drove back, aided by the guns of Fort St. Antoine. The Republicans retreated eastward leaving a few prisoners in the hands of the English. As they discovered the Spanish column under Gravina, supported on the right by the Neapolitans who approached up the Valbourdin, they saw the possibility of their being cut off and quickened their march eastward. The English learned from the prisoners that the French, about 1500 strong were drawn up on the eastern end of Faron. They continued along the ridge to Valbourdin, and found Victor's force arranged in the form of a triangle one side facing west, the other south.

The *redoute* of Faron lined with men, was in his rear, and between this *redoute* and his lines was placed the reserve. The valley Valbourdin widens off to the south-east in descending and thus protected Victor's left flank. Mulgrave got his men under cover before the narrow ridge, about 15 yards wide, which connects the height east and west of Valbourdin. To attack the French he had to cross this valley. It was decided to send Gravina, who had been approaching on the west side of Valbourdin, across to the east to attack the left of the enemy. He turned off to the right, but in starting to cross he received a heavy fire from the French. This forced him to cross further down.

The English waited for him to take up his position against the left of the enemy. This he did, following his advanced guard which was led by a Spanish sergeant who greatly distinguished himself. At first the left of Victor's force was exposed to a flank fire from the English and he moved part of it around to the right. As Gravina's column came up

Victor's left had to be protected again and reinforced. When Gravina engaged it, it began to waver, and by doing so gave the English and Piedmontese the signal to advance over the narrow pass. This double attack by a superior force was too much for the French. They broke and retreated in the wildest disorder.

The two attacking columns entered the *redoute* of Faron at the same moment. The French were pursued and many of them were dashed to pieces in falling over the cliffs. The small English force in Fort Faron seized this chance to fall upon the flank of the retreating Frenchmen. Victor with the few men he was able to keep around him, retreated in good order. In spite of his defeat he was the hero of the day:

> *Le chef de bataillon Victor, à qui on avait confié ce poste s'est conduit à merveille et dans l'occupation et dans la resistance qu'il a faite; il a été nommé chef de brigade, une voix unanime s'est levée pour lui.*

One of the English officers wrote:

> A M. Victor is said to have been killed. He was reckoned a good officer and all his dispositions that day were in the style of a man who understood his business.

Victor distinguished himself later on during the siege. The Republican loss on this day is very hard to give. The Allies lost about 100 men. Gravina was wounded "in the course of his able and spirited exertions at the head of the Neapolitans grenadiers."

All the troops fought well, writes Mulgrave, "I should do injustice, should I particularize any corps or any nation." The retaking of Mount Fafon was very important to the Allies. "Hood was glad it was as it gave an opportunity of recovering it so handsomely." [25]

This failure on the part of La Poype increased the ill-feeling between him and Carteaux. [26] Carteaux relieved him of his command. La Poype however was the brother-in-law of Fréron, the *Representant du peuple*, and for this reason he was soon reinstated. From now up to the end of October the Republican army was in the most pitiable state [27]; there was jealousy between the commanding generals, and ill-will between Carteaux and the *Representants*. On Oct. 12 Salicetti wrote "*Carteaux a besoin, outre la bonne volonté, des moyens personnels, et*

25. For the attack on Faron. *Memoires de Thaon; de Victor.* Letters from Graham. Mulgrave in *Gazette.* Letter from Hood, in *Admirals' Dispatches, Mediterranean* 1793, R. O. *Lettre de Gasparin et Salicetti* Oct. 4. R. A.
26. *Lettre Carteaux a La Poype.* Oct. 3. A. G.
27. *Lettres de Ricord*, Oct. 8: de Salicetti, Oct. 10, 12, 23, 27: *de Fréron*-Oct 20. R. A.

*nous ne lui connaissons pas d'autres que sa reputation."*

On Oct. 6th Carteaux wrote [28]

*Mais dites au Ministre, vous qui connaissez ma franchise que si l'on croit quelqu'un plus capable que moi pour remplir cette mission, que c'est avec reconnaissance que je céderai un fardeaux que la trahison la plus noire m'a rendu insupportable, car quel nom voulés vous que je donne à une Phrase qui dit tout simplement que je l'eusse voulu les Anglais ne seraient plus à Toulon et que peut penser de moi le comité de Salut Public, a qui l'on fait entendre que c'est pour avoir rejetté son plan que les Anglais ne sont pas chassés.*

The Republican soldiers were raw recruits, uncertain, undisciplined and poorly armed; many of the troops who arrived had no arms at all. [29] Salicetti and Gasparin went themselves to Marseilles and with great difficulty obtained 3000 guns. The one redeeming feature of the Republican army was the artillery. [30] Napoleon showed the greatest activity, collecting cannon, powder, and material of every kind. He was untiring in his efforts and definite in his purpose. His first two batteries have already been spoken of. *La Montague* opened fire on Sept 18; *Les Sans Culottes*, on the 20th.

*Située au bord de la mer à la pointe du Brégaillon; elle a fait son effet, elle a chasssé tous les pontons, les bombardes et les frégates qui se tenaient sur la gauche de l'Eguillette.*

These two batteries cleared the Petite Rade north of l'Eguillette. The village La Seyne was thus protected. The next battery, *Les Sablettes* was erected against Fort Mulgrave, which continued to be Napoleon's object of attack. *Les Sablettes* opened fire on Oct. 7

The Allies decided to attack it. They had learned from a deserter who knew the watchword, that it was defended by troops of the last conscription. At half past two in the morning of Oct 9, 400 English and Spanish left Fort Mulgrave to attack the battery. Led on by a French deserter, who answered the sentinels, they entered the battery; the first sentinel was killed, all who resisted were bayoneted. The enemy was completely routed, after making a short stand. They numbered about 300. The English spiked the guns, sawed the gun-carriages and destroyed the ammunition which was found in quantities

28. *Lettre de Carteaux à l'adjoint du Mtre de la Guerre, Archives de la Guerre.*
29. *Lettre de Veyrenne à Carteaux* Oct. 6. *Lettre de Carteaux au Ministre de la Guerre.* Oct. 7. *Proclamation de Carteaux.* Oct. 8. *Archives de la Guerre.*
30. *Lettres de Carteaux.* Sept. 29. Oct. 18. A. G. *Lettre de Salicetti* Sept. 25. A. G.

At 4 o'clock they marched back, having lost but four men killed and seven wounded. The Republicans lost seven men killed and ten wounded; also a few prisoners among them three officers and the lieutenant of artillery who commanded the battery. The damage was not very great.

*A trois heures après midi la batterie se trouve parfaitement rétablie et en état de jour. Vous avez ci-joint des proclamations que les enemis ont laissées en profusion en abandonnant la batterie. Nos soldats ne croient pas au tendre intérét des puissances coalisées pour la dynastie que nous avons culbuté due trone.*

[31]Napoleon's activity continued, new batteries were constantly being erected. Hood's record for these days is full of "heavy cannonading between the ships and batteries." "The enemy's gun and mortar Batteries are constantly playing upon our posts and shipping without our having the means of driving them to a greater distance." [32] At this time the Allied forces amounted to about twice the number of the besieging army: their troops were undoubtedly better. Why they did not make some successful sallies is hard to explain. In the meantime however the number of conscripts raised in the Var amounted to about 13,000 young men; and fresh battalions arrived daily. Were they all armed, it would perhaps have been possible to have made an attack one of the posts. As it was, the artillery was the only arm which annoyed the Allies in the least. The Petite Rade was gradually cleared of the ships, which were taken back to a safer position.

On Oct. 13th. news arrived of the fall of Lyons. The besieging army celebrated it in true republican style. Extra rations of *eau-de-vie* were distributed. There was dancing, music and singing. Whole battalions danced around in rings. The news was announced to the town by the shot and shell from a new battery which Napoleon had just completed: *Bréguart*, about 300 yards south of *Les Sablettes* "*elle balaye les rives de la droite de l'Eguillette et toute cette partie de la Grande Rade.*" [33] The Allies decided to stop this rejoicing and the next day, they made a sortie. Thaon de Revel termed it "*une étourdie militaire.*" At 11 o'clock in the morning 3000 of the Allies took up a defensive position behind the Riviere Neuve. 100 men were sent out to Hauteur des Arennes

---

31. Attack of Sablettes. Gasparin. Oct 7. R. A. *Memoires de Napoléon Mulgrave* in *Gazette.* Hood in *Gazette.*

32. Letter from Hood to John Trevor. Public Record Office. Foreign Office. Sardinia. 1793. Oct to Dec. Letters from Trevor to Grenville.

33. *Correspondance de Napoléon.*

to discover the movements of the enemy. A patrol of 800 men was sent out on the left. These advance bodies got too far forward and in protecting their retreat a general action came on.

The Allies retired to their position, and awaited the attack of the Republicans, but as night came on they retired to Fort Malbousquet. In giving an account of this engagement Carteaux praised Almeras highly. [34] "*L'intelligence et les talents du citoyen Almeras ont forcé nos ennemis à se reployer*". He did not mention Bonaparte, nor can I find anywhere a justification for Chuquet's saying that he led the troops on this day.[35] Carteaux praised the work of the batteries in the same letter, however:

> *Tant qu'à nos Batteries elles font le meilleur effet possible surtout la batterie des Sans-culottes . . . elle coupe de temps en temps quelques mats et maltraite les fréegates.*

The next day, October 15, it was the Republican's turn to take the offensive. Lapòype made an attack on Cap Brun,[36] but after a stubborn fight was driven back. The post was supposed to be in safety, but before long a second and much stronger column advanced, covered by the artillery. This time the Allies were soon driven from the post; four English officers fell in defending it. Once more a hurried Council of War was held at Toulon on the news of the loss of the post.

> *On délibéra à Toulon si l'on attaquerait le Cap Brun de vive force, ou si l'on obligerait l'ennemi a l'évacuer par un mouvement qui menaça de les envelopper.*

It was decided to outflank the Republicans. The position of the enemy was reconnoitred and it was found that they had abandoned Cap Brun, forming their whole line on a height further to the east, their left covered by Castle Ste Marguerite, which had two twelve pounders turned toward the land. Field pieces could be seen well distributed along the front of the enemy's line. The Allies marched under the protection of the guns of Fort Faron to La Vallette, leaving behind them 140 men with two 18 pounders, who with the guns from Fort Faron were to block the Vallon Favières and prevent the enemy from sending reinforcements by this pass from their post at Tourris and Revest. From La Vallette, they started for the Hauteurs de Thouars, a position commanding La Garde, and which would have given the allies control

---

34. *Correspondance de Carteaux au M. de la Guerre*, Oct. 18, A. G.
35. Chuquet—page 188.
36. Attack on Cap Brun. Thaon. Elphinstone in *Gazette*.

of the entire plain and of all the roads to the east of Toulon.

From this position the Republicans might have been forced miles away from the east side of the city. The Republicans saw their danger and moved in all haste from their position toward La Garde. Owing to the mistake of the guide, and to the rather slow manoeuvres of the Spanish and Neapolitan infantry which headed the column, the Republicans reached La Garde at the same time as the Allies gained the heights of Thouars. The battle now resolved itself into a heavy cannonade from each side.

> *Les Français firent un mouvement comme pour couper aux alliés le chemin de Toulon mais leur cavalerie mise en désordre par le canon, se retire bientôt. Les dragons de la Reine espagnole manoeuvrirent avec audace et succès.*

160 of these cavalrymen had just arrived three days before. When night came on the noise of the artillery and wagons leaving La Garde was distinctly heard, and as the Republicans did not answer the heavy guns of the allies, it was supposed that they had evacuated the place. A few men were sent ahead *"pour s'en assurer, mais le feu violent qui en partit, fit connaître qu'il était encore occupé"*. The object of the allies had been accomplished and they returned to Toulon. This was the only fight around Toulon of skilful manoeuvring where all three arms were employed.

The operations dragged on slowly, but the outlook for the Republicans was not bright. Fréron and Barras wrote from Marseilles:

> *A present les ennemis se sont renforcés et se renforcent tous les jours. Carteaux n'a aucune des connaissances militaires propres à s'emparer d'une des places les mieux fortifiées de la Republique*

Reinforcements were looked for from Toulon. In these days of depression Bonaparte was the only one who was active. On October 18th he opened a new battery, *"Des 4 Moulins, situee a 700 toises de la redoute anglaise."*[37] For the same day, can be read in Hood's *Journal*: "A heavy fire commenced from Hauteur de Grasse and ships in the N.W. Arm." The garrison of Fort Mulgrave began to see the danger of their position. For three days they kept up a continual fire on Napoleon's batteries, but failed to destroy any of them. And on October 22 they were attacked by still another; La Grande Rade, *"elle fait le même effet que celle du Bréguart"*. Hood's attention was continually called to Fort Mulgrave.

---

37. *Correspondance de Napoléon.*

On October 23 he wrote in his *Journal*; "Made the General signal to assist Camel with boats". This short sentence is proof that the Camel approached too close to Bonaparte's battery. About this time the powder became rather scarce and the batteries were not so noisy. In the meantime Napoleon was busily employed on four or five new ones; all in different stages of completion.

The constant yet somewhat unjust complaints against Carteaux had at last taken effect, and on October 21 he received notice that he was to be replaced at Toulon by General Doppet, who had commanded at Lyons. From now on until the departure of Carteaux on November 7 the siege rather dragged, although the monotony was broken now and then by a day of "heavy cannonading", as it was termed in Hood's *Journal*. No great harm seems to have been done. On October 30th the *Terrible* "signalled for assistance," but in general the ships keep at a safe distance. The last week in October troops and cannon began to arrive from Lyons and Grenoble, as well as many troops from the new levies; for the *Representants* were quite busy dispatching raw and useless recruits to the walls of Toulon.[38]

On October 25 Salicetti and Gasparin received news from Doppet informing them that he had sent off 3,000 troops. As they had expected 20,000 this information gave them a good deal of alarm, which they quickly made known to *the Comité de Salut public*. The Allies also received reinforcements, which added to the discouragement of the Republicans. Discipline in the Republican army was still bad and desertion frequent. At last on November 5 some good troops arrived from Lyons. Two days afterwards Carteaux left, complaining bitterly against Doppet *"qui n'a point de talents militaires,"* [39] and against Lapòype *"qui s'est conduit de manière a faire soupçonner sa fidelité."*[39]

He accused even the *Representants*; something which was very dangerous to do in that day.

*Quel rôle me fait-on jouer? Les forces de Lyons devoient sans retard marcher sur Toulon, il semble qu'une main les retienne et je suis obligé de surveiller jour et nuit une troupe fatigué de trois mois de Bivouac, et lorsque les moyens d'agir avec efficacité arriveront ceux qui m'ont liés les bras viendront pour que je leur cède la place, ils se sont bien gardés de hater les secours—ils n'ont écouté que leur ambition et la chose publique ne pouvant être sauvé par eux, ils n'ont pas voulu qu'un brave*

---

38. Letters under date of November 2. A. G. Letters from Oct. 22 to Nov. 5 from *Representants*. R. A.

39. *Lettre de Carteaux au Ministre de la Guerre.* Nov. 5th. A. G.

*homme la sauve.* [40]

Carteaux was quite right in saying that he was being removed just at the moment when things were taking a brighter turn. [41]

On Nov 5th. the Minister of War sent word to Doppet that he was to go to the Pyrenees: Carteaux was to be put in command of the Army of the Alpes to hold the Piedmontese in check: and General Dugommier was to take command at Toulon. [42] Doppet did not arrive until the 13th. From the 6th until this time Lapòype held the command. The real head of the army however was Salicetti, with whom at this time Napoleon had the greatest influence. He therefore practically had his hands free and if he felt that he was himself capable of directing an attack on Toulon he might through the influence of Salicetti attempt it; in spite of the fact that Doppet had given Lapòype instructions to remain on the defensive. [43] It seems in reality as if such an attack was made although it is impossible to get positive proof of it. The following is found in Pon's *Memoires.* It is said to have happened on Nov. 9;

> *La matinée l'ennemi attaquait le camp Balaguier mais sans succes. L'après-midi il feignait de marcher sur Malbousquet et Saint-Antoine dans le temps que le Général Lapòype simulait une attaque contre le Cap Brun. puis tout à coup se porta de nouveau sur Belaguier avec 1200 à 1500 hommes et fit encore une fois contraint de se retirer. Il revint à la charge ver les sept heures du soir avec 2000 à 3000 hommes. Le camp menacé venait de recevoir des troupes fraîches et des munitions. On laissa les republicans s'approcher des retranchements et au moment ou ils croyaient se rendre maîtres un feu très vif de mousqueterie et une décharge à mitrallle de l'artillerie les forcèrent à abandonner précipitamment le champ de bataille qui resta couvert de inorts et de blesses.*

This is rather a circumstantial account and is strengthened by the following which Salicetti wrote on Nov. 9th. [44]

> *Il nous arrive enfin des munitions, des pieces d'artillerie de l'armée de Lyon. . . . nous sorames maîtres d'une position où nous sommes occuper à nous fortifier, d'où nous pourrons incendier les édefices de l'infame Toulon, en les designant au doigt . . . on se prépare à attaquer les ennemis en même temps dans la rade, dans la ville et dans plusieurs forts.*

40. *Lettre de Carteaux à l'Adjoint au Ministre de la Guerre.* Nov. 4. A.
41. *Lettre de Salicetti.* Nov 9. R. A.
42. *Mtre. de la Guerre au Gen. Doppet.* Nov. 5. A. G.
43. *Lettre Salicetti.* Nov. 9. R. A. 21923
44. *Recueil Aulard.*

In other words Salicetti said they had just received more muni-
tions and artillery, that they occupied a strong position; (he must have
referred to the heights upon which the Battery, the Convention, was
situated, and that they were planning the very kind of an attack which
according to Pons was made.)

In Hood's *Journal—Nov 9.*

*Terrible* made signal for assistance, made *Royal* and *Robust* signals
for their boats to go to the assistance of the *Terrible.*

Here at least is proof that the attack upon the Rade was made. It
seems quite probable that this was the work of Bonaparte who had
induced Salicetti to risk an attack. As Lapòype and probably all the
officers were involved in it; as it was a failure; and as it was carried
out against orders, it is not surprising that there should be no official
account of it. The affairs of the Republican Army were carried on in
such a loose manner, that even such an attack might be passed over
without being noticed. The attack was, according to Pons' description,
a spirited one, but it proved somewhat premature and at all events a
failure. During this period before the arrival of Doppet, Napoleon
had been especially active in the erection of batteries: the material for
these was furnished by Lyons and Grenoble. On Nov. 9th. Salicetti
wrote:

*On terminera la nuit prochaine une batterie qui produira dans la
Grande Rade le même effet que les Sans-Culottes dans la Petite.*

Nov 12. [45]

*le 22 au 23 Brumaire la batterie des Sablettes a fait une feu terrible
sur la redoute des Anglais, a fait sauter un magazin à poudre et tué
beaucoup de monde par l'eclat des bombes qui ont pris feu. Demain
une nouvelle batterie, dite les hommes-sans-peur fera feu sur la Batterie
ennemi, une autre dite la convention nationale battera Malbousquet.*

Nov 13th: [46]

*On travaille avec ardeur à la construction de nouvelles batteries. A
l'arrivée du général nous ésperons de frapper de grands coups et d'avoir
des nouvelles importantes à vous communiquer.*

Hood wrote on Nov 13th. [47]

. . . . .their batteries approach by degrees both toward the town

45. *Lettre Salicetti.* Nov 12th. *Archives de la Guerre.* (Not published in *Recueil Aulard.*)
46. *Lettre Salicetti.* R.A.
47. Letter to John Trevor. Record Office. Sardinia.

and the fleet and it is of the highest importance that the garrison should be made strong enough to go out and destroy their works"

As is seen, by the arrival of Doppet Bonaparte's branch of the army had made the greatest progress: Napoleon had selected the position of, and started to erect, every battery which was used up to the fall of Toulon. [48] Therefore to him and to him alone belongs the credit of the principal arm of the besieging army at Toulon.

Doppet arrived on November 13th. He saw at once that he did not possess the necessary qualifications for carrying on a siege such as that of Toulon and Consented to stay only if it would be under the orders of Dugommier. Luck would have it however that the few days in which he was in command were rather exciting ones.

On November 15 an engagement took place. The following is Napoleon's account of it. [49]

> The soldiers of the battalion Côte d' Or stationed opposite Fort Mulgrave, seeing the Spaniards ill-treat a French prisoner, seize their arms and rush to his assistance. Other battalions follow and soon a whole division is engaged. Doppet and Bonaparte rush to the Scene. "*Le vin est tiré, il faut le boire*" says Napoleon in advising Doppet rather to continue the action than to withdraw the troops. Doppet allows him to direct the attack. Bonaparte places himself at the head of the *tirailleurs* who cover the hill, and forming two columns tries to penetrate into the Fort at its gorge.
>
> O'Hara, the Governor of Toulon, sees the action and hastens to Fort Mulgrave to urge on his troops, he makes a sortie which is vigorously supported by a cannonade from the ships and Fort. Doppet, seeing one of his aids killed at his side, gives the signal for retreat. Napoleon is furious and galloping toward Doppet exclaims, "*Toulon est manqué, et un . j— . — . . . a fait battre la retraite.*"

Such is Napoleon's account which Cottin[50] puts aside, and then relates how it was "*en réalité.*" In the War Archives a contempory and detailed report of this engagement exists and I shall give it about in full. It will be seen that it is quite reconcilable with Napoleon's account.

*Rapport du Citoyen Brulé, Chef du 2[ie] Bon de la Côte d'Or, com-*

---

48. Letter Nov 14th. *Correspondance de Napoléon*. Here the future position of every battery afterwards erected is mentioned.
49. Salicetti. November 17th. R. A. *Memoires de Napoléon*.
50. Cottin. page 266.

40

*mandant la division ditte de la Plaine à l'armée Revolutionnaire près Toulon. Le 25e jour du 2° Mois de la de année 2 de la Republique française une patrouille ennemie s'étant présentée devant la Seine nos postes avancées furent à sa rencontre. Le combat s'engage entre elles. Ces patrouilles se grossirent de Part et d'autre de manière qu'au bout de trois quarts d'heures on eut dît que c'était deux armées au lieu de Patrouilles. Moi sousigné m'étant transporté sur les lieux je ralliai les troupes de la Republique et ordonnai la charge. Alors nos troupes fondèrent sur l'ennemi avec un tel acharnement que je ne pus les empecher d'aller jusqu'a la redoute ennemie. M'y étant transporté moi-même je jugeai qu'il aurait été imprudent de tenter un assaut puisque ce poste ne nous aurait été d'aucune utilité pour le moment attendu l'impossibilité de pouvoir le conserver. En consequence je ordonnai la retraite qui s'effectua dans le meilleur ordre possible. Nous avons perdus dans cette affaire qu'a duré 5 heures 10 à 12 hommes qui sont morts sur le champ de bataille et environ 15 blessés. . . . L'ennemi a eu environ 60 ou 70 hommes tués dont la pluspart out été tués dont leur redoute, nous leur avons fait aussi un prisonnier.* [51]

---

51. Cottin's authorities are Thaon de Revel: *Boullement de Lachenaye. Journal de Vernes. Raports Napolitains.* (He admits that the *Journal de Vernes* is inexact: Thaon de Revel's account does not conflict with Napoleon's: I found the *Raports Napolitains* in London, but put them aside as scanty and containing nothing of value). With these Cottin relates how it was *"en réalité."* Napoleon's account is corroborated by the report of Brulé, the account of Doppet (letter Nov 17th. *Archives de la Guerre*) and a letter from O'Hara under date of Nov 15th. in the *Gazette.* Attacks on this day were frequent. Doppet writes, *"L'ennemi voyant commencer des travaux trop près de lui et s'élever des batteries qui rendroient la prise des siennes moines difficiles a pris le parti de faire à chaque instant des sorties du côté de nos travailleurs"*. . . *"Le même jour (15th Nov.) nous avons été attaqué à notre droite du côté des Sablettes au centre du côté de Malbousquet, et à la gauche du côté du fort St. Antoine. non contentes de les repousser, nos troupes ont à la gauche et à la droite poursuivi l'ennemi jusque dans ses retrenchements, cependant cette affaire étant générale n'ayant eu ni donné aucune plan d'attaque, les forces étant de plus trop divisées pour en esperer en avançant des avantages reels et durables chaque chef de colonne fit engager ses postes à sa troupe"*. This shows that Doppet had no plan of attack, that each *chef* directed his own affair, and that regarding the engagements in such a light, it is quite possible that Doppet sounded the retreat when he found his soldiers too far advanced. Cottin says the *"l'objectif réel des republicans était toujours Balaguier, centre lequel Doppet lança d'abord 50, puis 500, enfin 1500 hommes"*. The attack on Balaguier was the all important one, but it was not Doppet who directed it, nor were the other attacks false ones, made by Doppet, as Cottin puts it. Napoleon took part in the attack of Balaguier, and nothing can be found to disprove his account of it.

O'Hara writes, "Mulgrave vigorously and repeatedly attacked by a large corps of the enemy."

Here the chief of the Battalion Cote d'Or admits that his men got away from him, and it is quite possible that while he was sounding the retreat, Napoleon was trying to form the scattered, but still advancing troops into column to enter the fort. It is also not surprising that Napoleon thought Doppet had given orders to sound the retreat; which he may also have done.

CHAPTER 3

# Bonaparte's Plan

On Nov. 17 Dugommier arrived. He was far a better general than Carteaux, Lapòype, or Doppet. Fifty-five years old, he had seen some service. He was formally an officer in a marine battery; he took part with some distinction in the Seven Years War, and also in the American War of Independence. Then he retired to his estate in the West Indies, from whence he had been sent as a deputy to Paris; later he re-entered the army, was made brigadier general in Oct. 1792. In the Italian army he likewise distinguished himself, became general of division: in short he was a good soldier.

An old artillery general, Du Theil, arrived two hours after Dugommier. Doppet and Albitte had brought him to take charge of the artillery, but he was forced to remain a few days in Marseilles, and consequently did not arrive with Doppet. About this time a decided and continual improvement took place in the condition of the besieging army. Reinforcements, artillery and ammunition arrived in great quantity: these came principally from Lyons. The taking of this city had a great effect upon the attack of Toulon, as it permitted about all the forces employed there to be turned against the Allies in Toulon. There was however difficulty in finding provisions for the Republican army, and toward the end of the siege this question became one of great importance. [1]

On Nov. 24 the *chef de bataillon*, Marescot, a friend of Carnot's arrived, *"pour diriger le génie"*. The next day he wrote to Carnot;

> *J'ai été visiter les attaques qui ne sont autre chose que quelques batteries provisoires dressées par les officiers d'artillerie destinées à combattre les batteries avancées des rebelles et à favoriser les premières operations qui*

---

1. *Lettres de Salicetti*, Nov. 9 to 13. R. A.

*doivent avoir lieu le plus tôt possible.* [2]

This was his first impression, a little later he wrote somewhat differently. On Jan 9th. 1794 in a *Relation de la prise de Toulon* he wrote:

> . . . .*nos dispositions d'attaque n'étaient autre chose que des batteries provisoires placées avantageucement par le chef de bataillon Bonaparte, commandant en second de l'artillerie.* [3]

Here he admitted that the batteries were placed "*avantageusement*" and by Bonaparte. His terming them "*batteries provisoires*" was quite wrong; he probably meant that in their construction they had not all the complete details such as would appeal to the eyes of an engineer. This was the case, but under the circumstances (dirth of workmen etc.) was quite unavoidable. It will be seen what success the engineers had in trying to complete these batteries. Their positions were their strong points and, as it has been seen, the course of the siege proved this to Marescott.

On Nov 25th. Dugommier held a council of war: the *Representants*, the generals, Bonaparte, Marescot and others were present There has been a good deal written about the plan of attack followed at Toulon; attempts made to prove that Napoleon was its originator, as well as to prove the contrary; yet no one seems to have laid stress upon the fact that on Nov 14, therefore 10 days before the council of war, Bonaparte in a letter to the Minister of War, [4] proposed a plan of attack which corresponded in almost every detail with that decided upon in the Council: As Napoleon drew up the *procès verbal* of the council, both the plans are published in his *Correspondance*.

The war council decided: to make the principal attack on Eguillette:[5] to attack Malbousquet with the batteries la Convention and la Poudriere, so to deceive the enemy as to the point of attack, and to prepare the way for the infantry "*si les evenements en permettent l'attaque*": to establish a battery against Cap Brun to deceive the enemy as to the point of attack; to take Faron: all attacks were to be made at the same time: the "*division de droite*" was to attack Eguillette and to make a false attack on Malbousquet (this "false" attack was to be carried out if possible) the "*division de gauche*" was to make the attack on Faron and a false attack on Cap Brun. Much of the plan related to

2. Letter from Marescot. Nov 25th. R. A.

3. *Relation de la prise de Toulon, écrit le 9 Janvier 1794. par le Général Marescot, Archives de la Guerre.*

4. *Correspondance de Napoléon.*

5. *Lettre 25 Novembre. Correspondance de Napoléon.*

the batteries.

It was decided; to erect batteries "*à l'extremité du promontoire de l'Eguillette, afin d'obliger l'escadre à évacuer la rade et même de la brûler, si un vent contraire s'oppose à sa sortie*": to erect one against Cap Brun; another "*de 6 mortiers à grande portée centre Toulon*" between la Convention and Malbousquet: to establish a "*redoute de protection sur la gauche de la montagne de la Convention pour empêcher que l'ennemi favorisé par le feu des redoutes de Sainte Antoine ne tourne et n'elève la batterie de la Convention*". Napoleon wrote in his above mentioned letter of Nov 14th.

> *Chasser les ennemis de la rade est le point préliminaire . . . . pour se rendre maître de la rade il faut se rendre maître de la pointe de l'Eguillette. Au même moment que nous serions maîtres de la pointe de l'Eguillette, il faudrait bombarder Toulon avec 8 ou 10 mortiers. Nous sommes maîtres de la hauteur des Arènes qui n'en est pas à 900 toises et nous pourrons facilement nous approcher à 800 toises sans passer la rivière Neuve: dans le même temps l'on placerait deux batteries devant le fort Malbousquet, et une contre le fort l'Artigues. . . . Aujourd'hui il serait possible que quoique la flotte fut obligé d'évacuer la rade la garnison tînt encore et soutînt le siège.*
>
> *Alors les 2 batteries que nous aurions établis contre Malbousquet seraient promptement renforcées par une troisième: les mortiers qui pendant 3 jours auraient bombardé Toulon se tourneraient pour ruiner les défenses de Malbousquet. Le fort ne résistera pas 48 heures et rien ne nous arrête alors jusqu'au front de Toulon. Nous attaquons le front composé par le bastion du Marais et le bastion de l'arsenal par une attaque brusquée qui nous conduit tout de suite à la deuxieme parallèle favorisés par les batteries placeés au Malbousquet et par celles placées sur le revers des Arénes. Nous serions génés dans cette opération par le fort l'Artigues mais 4 mortiers et les 6 pièces de canon qui y aurait été placés au premier moment de l'attaque, y resteraient et feraient alors un feu plus vif. . . .*

Then he continued "*La prise de l'Eguillette, l'expulsion des Anglais des rades et le bombardement et dans le même temps attaquer le Faron*".

From carefully comparing these two plans, it will be seen that Napoleon's was practically the same as the one decided upon in the council of war. Napoleon did not speak of the false attack against Cap Brun, and proposed batteries to be erected against Fort Artigues and not against the *redoute* Sainte Antoine, as it is mentioned in the final plan. With these two exceptions they are about identical. This shows conclusively that Napoleon was quite decided as to the proper plan of attack before the arrival of Dugommier. It is wrong however to say that Bonaparte was the sole originator of this plan, or to attribute any great merit to him if he had been.

There were at least three vital points around Toulon; the most vital was certainly Fort La Malgue; this the Republicans could not well attack as it was strong for two reasons: the English had first landed there, and used it as a point of protection for their fleet; again all the forts on the east side of Toulon had been better built, as it was from the east that any possible land attack on Toulon was supposed to come. Faron was also a position of great importance.

This had been recognized at once by the Republicans, but their attack upon it had failed in the end. Lastly the Eguillette: this was also a splendid point of attack and the easiest to approach. Napoleon had recognized this immediately; but any well instructed officer would have done so. That Carteaux, who understood nothing about the use of artillery and whose tactics consisted in using the *bayonette*, had not seen this, is not so surprising.

Someone had however sent this advice, the attacking of Eguillette, from Paris. Salicetti wrote on Sept 26th. to the *Comité du Salut Public*,[6] accusing Carteaux for having allowed the English to get possession of Eguillette.

*Le général que nous avions cru comprendre et adopter notre plan n'y avait aucune confiance quoique celui que vous avez envoyé de Paris fût exactement le meme.*

On Sept 25th. he wrote to the Minister of War.

*Nous l'aurions forcé de quitter la rade, si ce général avait voulu executer le plan que nous lui avons proposé et qui etait celui du Comité de Salut Public.*[7]

The idea of attacking the Eguillette came therefore from Paris. Bonaparte, as was natural had seen that it was the best point to attack and his batteries were erected against it, and did the greatest part toward taking it. The Republican Army had however, after the council of war, a plan which was agreed upon by all; it was no longer Bonaparte's idea only. Everyone went to work to carry it out. The condition of the army was however far from satisfactory in many ways. Barras wrote from Marseilles on Nov 19th. "*La situation de l'armée n'est*

6. *Recueil Aulard.*
7. *Archives de la Guerre.*

*pas satisfaisant.*"

Victor said in his *Memoires:*

*Notre armée était jeune, pleine d'ardeur, mais il n'était point facile de la soumettre aux lois d'une exacte discipline.*

Marescot *le chef du génie*, had the greatest difficulty in trying to carry out his elaborate plans of a *"siège en règle"*. The workmen were wanting, implements were hard to obtain, and he met with little encouragement on all sides. Finally however he became convinced that one must proceed in the most practical manner, and get along without that which it was impossible to obtain: but when at last, he was convinced of this fact the siege was about over; consequently Marescot, even as *chef du génie*, had no influence upon the direction of the siege. Dec 10 he wrote:

*. . . . je vois que chacun ici est persuadé qu'il ne sera pas nécessaire de devellopper des attaques réguliéres pour reduire Toulon, j' aime à le croire et même je le presume.*

And after frequent complaints to his friend Carnot of the insufficiency of the material necessary for his branch of the army he ended by admitting that up to Dec. 10 he had done nothing.[8] Those who strive to diminish the role of Bonaparte at Toulon lay stress upon the fact that Marescot arrived at the same time as Dugommier; and to direct the siege.

One branch of the army continually and regularly increased, and that was the artillery. From now on to the end it will be seen how the Republican artillery kept up a constant and effective fire upon the entire western side of Toulon, until the Allied fleet sailed from the harbour in haste. Nelson wrote on Dec 1st.[9]

. . . . . shot and shells are very plentiful all over the harbour. I wonder more damage has not yet been done. General O'Hara I hope will be able to drive the French from the heights near the harbour or we shall be unpleasantly situated, not that I think Toulon is in the slightest danger. At all events we can destroy the French fleet and Arsenal in a very short time.

On Nov 28th the battery La Convention was opened upon Fort Malbousquet; it apparently did no very great damage; but its commanding position worried the Allies a great deal, and it was decided

---

8. *Marescot à Carnot.* Dec. 10th. *Archives de la Guerre.*
9. *Nelson's Dispatches.*

to make a sortie and try to destroy it. [10] About 3000 troops, British, Spanish, Neapolitan Piedmontese and French *refugies* left the garrison about four in the morning, and supported by field artillery and the guns of Malbousquet, marched upon the Hauteur des Arenes. The Republicans were taken more or less by surprise and driven back in great confusion. The Allies however instead of forming on the height and preparing themselves for a counter attack which was certain to come, pursued the French along the road towards Ollioules, or stopped to plunder. Even the spiking of the guns was carried out slowly and imperfectly.

The news of the success of the Allies was soon spread through the camp. General Garnier, who commanded in this division, was making a stubborn retreat with the few reliable men which he could gather around him, when Dugommier, Bonaparte and others soon came on the scene with reinforcements. The Allies were attacked with decision by superior forces, in the flank, and at a moment when they were in confusion. Threatened to be cut off from the town they retreated in great haste and disorder, the Republicans following close on their heels. The Piedmontese went back in less disorder than the others, and they were also about the only ones prepared to make a stand on the Heights: alone, however, they could do nothing.

The Allies brought their field pieces back from the Riviere Neuve with great difficulty, as the Republicans followed them so closely, and with such determination right up to the works of Malbousquet, which they tried to enter by repeated attacks. The guns of this fort and those of the Redoute Ste. Antoine forced them to retire. "*Le combat a été bien chaude*" wrote Salicetti; and Napoleon "*La matiné a été belle*". The fight was clearly to the advantage of the Republicans, as the Convention and three other batteries were blazing away harder than ever in a day or so; and the Allies in their attempt lost about 700 of their best troops killed, wounded, or taken prisoners: among the latter was General O'Hara and about 17 officers.

O'Hara was at first with the reserve on the Riviere Neuve, but after the Allies had taken the Convention, he advanced for some un-known reason to the battery, received a wound in the arm and as the

---

10. Attack on Convention. *Lettre du General Garnier*. Nov 30th. *Archives de la Guerre, Lettre de Salicetti*. Nov. 30th., Letter from Elliot, Thaon. Letter to Sir W. Hamilton, *Correspondence*. British Museum Mss. Egerton 2638, *Relation de Marescot. Lettre de Dugommier, Archives Nationales* A. F. 1,281, Letters from Hood and Dundas in Ga-zette.

Allies fell back he was left behind and a few Republican soldiers from the *bataillon d'Isere* made him prisoner.

It was not only around the Hauteur des Arènes but on the entire western side that the fight took place. The Republican batteries hurled shot at Fort Mulgrave and at the fleet, both of which answered in the most spirited manner. The artillery played an important part in driving the Allies back from the Convention, as well as in protecting Garnier's retreat at the beginning of the engagement. Just what part Napoleon took in this affair is hard to say, as accounts are so conflicting. But at all events there is absolute proof that he distinguished himself. [10]

> *Parmi ceux qui se sont le plus distingués et qui m'ont le plus aidé à rallier et à pousser en avant, ce sont le citoyens Buonaparte commandant l'artillerie, Arèna et Cervoni, adjudants généraux".* Salicetti wrote on this day, "*Le Général Mouret, Garnier et Buonaparte se sont dans cette occasion conduits d'une manière distinguee.* [11]

It will be noticed that he was mentioned by Dugomier first among those who aided him, and that by Salicetti he was mentioned with two of the generals, and lastly, that he is the only one who is named in both reports.

The next two weeks were spent in preparing the batteries and in frequent artillery duels. This arm had at last assumed most formidable proportions [12], thanks to the activity of Bonaparte in procuring material of every description from Marseilles, Lyons, Grenoble, Biancon, etc., and to his judgement in selecting the positions of his batteries. Victor wrote that by Dec. 6. 194 *bouches à feu* were turned against Toulon; "*or ces puissants moyens étaient dirigés par Bonaparte; car le Général Dutheil émervillé de la justesse et de la supériorité de ses vues s'était complement effacé devant lui*". [13] Some idea of the amount of work required in the artillery may be gathered from the following report of Dutheil to the Minister of War, on December 2nd. [14]

> *Personnel de l'artillerie—il faudrait 6 officiers supericurs, autants d'adjutants majors, undirecteur du Parc, un sous directeur, un commissaire des guerres un proposé du payeur general, 20 conducteurs des charrios il n'y a pas le quart de cannoniers necessaires. . . . il faudrait*

10. *Lettre de Dugommier*. Nov. 30. *Archives de la Guerre.*
11. *Lettre de Salicetti* Nov. 30 R. A.
12. Letter from O'Hara. *Archives Nationales* AF II 9.
13. *Memoires de Victor.*
14. *Archives de la guerre.*

*au moins 8 commissairesde plus. Les cannoniers auxiliaires n'ayant que de la valeur et aucune instruction. . . . Poudrede la Guerre—Gassendi chef de Bataillon envoyé par les representans du peuple dans toutes les places jusqu'à Metz et Strasbourg pour notre approvisionnement de siège anonce que c'est la partie qui nous rnanquera le plus, quelque soit ses efforts pour nous en procurer.*

The question of infantry cartridges was a most vital one. Bonaparte, and later Duteuil were loud in denouncing the wasteful expenditure here, especially in the affair of November 30. At last Salicetti took most severe measures for stopping this. Even as late as December 10 Dugommier wrote to the Minister of War:

*La poudre et les autres rnunitions de guerre exigent encore ta sollicitude. Je t'ai mandé que nous étions bien loin de la quantité calculée raisonablement et nécessaire à notre but.*

A day or so before the attack of the Convention three new batteries were opened. The *Convention*; the *Homme-sans-peur*, "*située sur un mamelon dominé par le camp Anglais* (Fort Mulgrave) *Le général en a arrêté la construction par ce qu'il croyait l'infanterie trop faible pour s'y soutenir*"; and the "*Petite Rade, destinée à éloigner les bâtiments de la côte et des voisinages de la poudrière*".[15] On December 1 the Poudriere opened fire on Malbousquet. "Observed a great deal of cannonading and musketry at the different posts and more especially near Fort Malbousque", Such was the account of it in Hood's *Journal*.

Dugommier became more and more enthusiastic over the artillery. On November 30 he wrote to the Minister of War:

*J'attends la perfection de deux batteries qui doivent jouer un beau role dans cette journée.* [16]

Dec. 4:

*Les batteries necessaires à l'execution du dernier plan sont presque entierement achevées - - - - - Nous sommes pauvres en artilleurs.*

Dec. 10:

*Chaque jour notre position s'ameliore par la perfection des batteries necessaires à l'attaque des postes exterieures qu'occupe l'ennerni et indiqués dans mon plan d'attaque. Je voudrais pouvoir t'en dire autant des autres moyens qui doivent contribuer à nos succes.*

About this time the batteries *La Farinière*, to the right of the *Con-*

15. *Correspondance de Napoléon.*
16. *Archives de la Guerre.*

*vention*, and *Jacobins* to the left of *Hommes-sans-Peur*, and directed against Fort Mulgrave, were opened on the enemy.

On Dec. 13, Lord Hood wrote that there was nothing of importance since the 30th of November, but that new batteries were going up on all sides, and that two of them "did us some mischief, on the 9th and 10th." "We shall soon have more men in the hospital than are fit for service". [17]

Dundas wrote on December 12:

> The enemy have increased number of mortars which have much annoyed our two posts of Cap Brun and Fort Mulgrave.[18]

On December 12 a new Council of War was held, where it was decided to continue the old plan. Dugommier, however, seemed to doubt its success; his views were too pessimistic for a good general. On December 13 he wrote to the *Comité*:

> *La moitié de cette armée est nulle, sans être connaisseur il ne faut que voir pour en être convaincu . . . . . Les officiers ne valent pas leur subordinés. Les trois quarts ne s'occupent que de leurs plaisirs et de la nouvelle existance dont ils jouissent.* [19]

Duteil seemed to be in the same state of uncertainty and on December 14 he wrote to the Minister of War telling of the canoniers which were wanting etc.[19] Napoleon was confident. And holding an important position in the principal arm of a great siege, with 64 officers and 1600 men under him, and but one old artillery general, with whom he was in the best understanding over him, seeing his many and well placed batteries taking a constantly increasing effect on the enemy he could not but feel certain of success.

On December 24 after the siege was over he wrote to Dupin "*Je t'ai annoncé de brillants succès et tu vois que je te tiens parole*". [20] On December 14 the final cannonading commenced, "A heavy cannonade from and against Fort Mulgrave" as Hood wrote in his *Journal*. The principal point of attack was Fort Mulgrave, and it was bombarded for three days. Thaon wrote:

> *Le feu était continuel et si violent que l'on comptait jusqu'à 7 bombes en l'air a la fois—La cannonade était violente. Tout était en jeu. La perte journalière était forte et les troupes harassées de fatigue. Un feu*

---

17. Hood in *Gazette* under date of December 13.
18. Dundas in *Gazette* under date of December 12.
19. *Correspondance de Napoléon.*
20. *Correspondance de Napoléon.*

*continuel de 5 batteries de canon et de mortiers durait depuis 3 jours et 3 nuits contre les ouvrages de Balaguier. On s'attendait a une attaque, on envoya un renfort de 350 hommes a Balaguier.'*

Further on he said *"les defenses avaient été fort endommagées par le feu ennemi"*

Victor wrote in his memoirs:

*. . . . l'ennemi ne restait point inactif. Après le feu terrible et continuel que l'on faisait depuis plusieurs jours sur ses postes principaux, il s'attendait à une attaque générale.*

Dundas wrote:

. . . works (of Mulgrave) suffered much. The number of men killed and disabled was considerable.[21]

Langara wrote that Fort Mulgrave:

. . . . which they had bombarded and cannonaded from different quarters with the utmost vivacity during the three preceding days[22] . . . .

Smith wrote: [23]

As a prelude to the general assault the enemy directed an uninterrupted fire of shot and shells against the Post of the Hauteur de Grasse for several days and nights. The troops being unsheltered from the shells suffered much and were so harassed that it. is not to be wondered at that they were not able to resist the attack.

I have quoted so much on the events and state of the army from the arrival of Dugommier up to the final attack on Fort Mulgrave, to show that in the siege of Toulon the artillery played by far the greatest part; that it was the one arm which inspired Dugommier with more or less confidence; that furthermore, it received from the corps of engineers under Marescot practically no support, and very little from the infantry, which was bad from the officers down; and that in the successful attack on Fort Mulgrave the greatest part of the credit falls to the artillery which for three days preceding had gradually destroyed the work and harassed the garrison to such an extent that they were driven out by inferior infantry, and in spite of the fact that an attack was expected.

---

21. Dundas to Henry Dundas, Dec. 20. *Correspondence of Smith-Barrow.*
22. Langara to Alcudia. Dec. 21 . St. Helens. R. O.
23. Smith to Hamilton. Dec. 24. *Correspondence of Smith-Barrow.*

The final attack on Fort Mulgrave took place on December 17.[24] It had a garrison of about 700 men, made up of English, Spanish and Neapolitans. On the evening of 16th, about 7,000 of the best Republican troops were gathered at La Seyne. The plan was to make the attack in two columns, of about 2,000 men each, with a third column of about the same number as a reserve. Victor commanded the column which was to move along the coast of the promontory and attacking the fort on its right side, cut off all help which might be sent from Balaguier or Eguillette. The second column commanded by Brulé was to march against the front of the *redoute*. The reserve column was to hold itself ready to come to the assistance of whichever column needed it. It was a very stormy night, and at the last moment there was some hesitation as to whether the attack should be delayed until the next day or not.

The *Representants* and Dugommier each seemed anxious to shift the responsibility. Bonaparte's advice was to go ahead, as bad weather was not at all disadvantageous for such an attack. The excitement caused by uncertainty and impatience at last seized them, and between one and two in the morning the signal was given. The plan of attack was quite forgotten. The fort was to be taken, and both columns, forming into one, rushed forward in the true Republican revolutionary manner straight for the fort. To the noise of the storm, the cannon, and the Marseillaise, was added at the first resistance the usual cries of *"sauve qui peut! à la trahison!"*

In this way the cowardly tried to excuse their dastardly retreat. The others, who were fortunately the greater part, pushed on up to the *redoute*, where they were met with a determined resistance. Victor was wounded, and already Dugommier cried *"je suis perdu!"* and started for the reserve column. It was already on its way, led on by Bonaparte and an artillery captain, Muiron, who knowing the ground well, lead the advance guard. By a third and last effort they entered the fort, and after a few minutes deadly fight in the dark, the enemy retreated to Balaguier and Eguillette.

24. For the final attacks, and departure of the Allies; *Memoirs de Victor*, Thaon, *Napoleon. Relation de Marescot*. Hood's *Journal*. Letters: *Salicetti à Albitte, Archives Nationales* AF II 2151 Langara to Alcudia, Dec. 21. St. Helens R. O. *Dugommier au M. de la Guerre* Dec. 18. A. G. Barras Dec. 16. A. G. and Dec. 18. *Recueil Aulard*. Dundas in *Gazette*. Cook to Auckland Dec. 20. and Elliot to same, Dec. 24 *Correspondence* Auckland. Hood to Henry Dundas Dec. 20; Smith to Hood Dec. 20; David Dundas to Henry Dundas Dec. 20; and Smith to Hamilton Dec. 24. *Correspondence of Smith-Barrow*. 2192-4

At 4 o'clock the news reached Hood that Fort Mulgrave was taken. Bonaparte put Marmont, the future *Duc de Raguse* in charge of the artillery of the captured post and directed him to turn the guns against the ships. In the morning when the other troops at Balaguier and Eguillette discovered the enemy in possession of Mulgrave they crowded "to the water like the herd of swine, that ran furiously into the sea possessed of the devil." [25] The ships and mortar boats of the Allies bombarded Fort Mulgrave, but before long the *Courageux* made the signal "wanting boat to tow". Smith wrote:

> The idea of *sauve qui peut* now seemed to possess everybody, the fleets of the different nations alarmed at the idea of being burnt by red hot shot or shells from Fort Mulgrave, Balaguier and Eguillette (now in possession of the enemy) weighed anchor and crowded out of the road in such haste as to alarm the troops on shore lest they should be left behind.

This same morning Faron was attacked on three sides at once, east, west and north. After some resistance and the usual "*sauve qui peut!*" and "*la trahison*", after which the cowardly no longer impeded the advance, the Republicans succeeded in establishing themselves there. "*Lapòype tant calomnieé s'est aussi parfaiternent bien comporte*". Thaon described this success as "*aussi funeste qu'incroyable*". Napoleon, after making his dispositions at Fort Mulgrave, proceeded to turn his batteries on Fort Malbosquet, for although he felt certain that the Allies would soon evacuate the city, he was determined that his shot and shells should hasten their departure.

Fréron wrote Dec 18:

> *Ils ont pris des mesures pour mettre leur flotte à l'abri de nos canons et de nos bombes qui n'ont cessé de les accablés.*

This constant artillery fire had a most demoralizing effect upon the Allies. In the night of the 17th. they abandoned Fort Malbousquet and Fort Pomets and very soon all the outside posts were in the hands of the Republicans except Fort Mulgrave which the Allies were forced to hold to protect the embarkation.

As soon as the news reached Hood that Mulgrave was taken a hurried council of war was called, on the morning of the 17th. Hood, Langara, Gravina, Dundas, Elliot, Thaon de Revel and others were present. The question was whether after the loss of Balaguier and Faron it was advisable to hold the town. Hood and Gravina, counting

---

25. Account of Sir Sidney Smith.

upon the reinforcements promised from Gibraltar, and on the 5000 Austrian troops who were on their way, voted for resistance, but gave in at last to the opinion of the majority; which was to abandon the city.

It was decided; that the garrisons of Malbousquet and Misiessy should hold out to the last extremity to cover the retreat; to inform the inhabitants that the powers would use all means to carry away those who desire to leave the city; to embark the sick and wounded at once; to carry off the French vessels which remained armed during the siege and to destroy the others, as well as the *magasins de la Marine* and the arsenal. Immediately afterwards preparations were made for the embarkation although it was not until the next morning, Dec. 18 that the time was set. At first the inhabitants of the town, kept in ignorance of the intended departure, were quiet and orderly. The next day things began to change.

As the Republicans drew nearer and nearer, as the troops were seen getting ready for departure in such large numbers, and especially as the shot and shell began to create havoc in the town and harbour, it dawned upon the inhabitants what was taking place. Then the wildest confusion reigned, some rushing to the shore for boats, others donning the red cockade, and vowing vengeance upon their fellow-citizens, who still remained royalists. Blood was shed in the streets between the rival factions. This state of affairs was rendered more terrible by the fire of the enemy.

It will be remembered that Napoleon turned his batteries against Malbousquet after the fall of Mulgrave. He had said, a month before, that under such conditions Malbousquet would not hold out 48 hours. That evening it was evacuated, in spite of the formal orders of the council of war, that it was to be held. The further work of the artillery is well described by Thaon de Revel.

*L'ennemi travailla à des batteries pendant tout la journée et la nuit (of the 17th) et les fit jour de bonne heure. (on the 18th) Les Français maîtres de l'artillerie qui était à Malbousquet canonnaient et bombardaient la ville. Ils avaient de même des encloué et tourné contre les Alliés toutes les bouches à feu des postes abandonnés. C'était un feu infernal et continuel contre la ville, la rade et le port.*

It was decided on the morning of the 18th to embark at 12 o'clock that night; but the constant advance of the Republicans upset the plans of the Allies somewhat and caused them to hasten their departure. [26] It took place in comparatively good order; the troops were all taken off without the loss of a man. This was not the case with the refugees; they hurried in large and terrified crowds to the water's edge: the war ships and all boats in the harbour were put at their disposal, but still many were lost in their wild flight by overcrowding the boats, and some of the boats were sunk by the shells of the enemy. The fact that 90 anchors were picked up in the harbour afterwards shows how quickly the boats must have departed. The whole affair was a terrible sight.

Elliot wrote to Lady Elliot Dec 20. "There has seldom been crammed more misery and more terror in a short space than we have witnessed these last four days" . . . Fortunately the weather was good. "Had the weather been such as it has been ever since that is to say blowing strong from the eastward we must have all, fleet, army and refugees inevitably perished". On the English and Spanish fleet were about 6000 refugees, who had been taken from the town. Some French accounts of Toulon contain long literary descriptions of the horrors of this day, and do not hesitate to follow them with a sharp condemnation of the action of the Allies, especially the English, in not taking off all the inhabitants.

In the first place all detailed accounts of these incidents are more or less untrustworthy; to discriminate between the behaviour of the Allies is quite wrong as no proof exists that the English were any less anxious to help the refugees than the Spaniards: they each had about an equal number on their fleets.

De Brècy, *directeur des douanes royales* at Toulon, who was one of the fugitives wrote:

> *L'Amiraux Hood, Goodal et Parker, Elliot et d'autres firent des offres les plus généreuses aux fugitifs. Le gouvernment Anglais payait en outre tous les secours accordés aux fugitifs à Livourne, l'île d'Elbe et la Corse.*

As to taking them all off on such short notice it was next to impossible. Again these writers might, with more justice and far greater success, criticise and condemn the cruelty of the Republican army which made such a measure necessary in a civilized country at the end of the 18th century. It is true that Fox criticised the action of the English bitterly, but it was part of the plan of the opposition.

---

26. Hood in *Gazette* under date Dec 20. "It became unavoidably necessary that the retreat should not be deferred beyond that night as the enemy commanded the town and ships by their shot and shell"

We do not know to what number but it is certain that thousands of poor wretches who have been deluded by our promises are now left by us to the guillotine. It must be a strong case of necessity which can justify such a proceeding . . .

One thing remained still to be done before leaving the city, namely, to burn or destroy the ships, which could not be taken away, and the Arsenal. Sir Sidney Smith and the adjutant of the Spanish navy were ordered to perform this duty. According to the agreement in the council of war it was to be done at the last moment, but they started either a little too late or the Republicans advanced a little too quickly. At all events Smith did not complete his work and the Spaniard did his stupidly.

As Smith approached the Arsenal, preparing to burn everything, he found a number of the inhabitants, principally prisoners who had liberated themselves, ready to dispute him. The shouts of the Republicans could be heard not far off and the musket balls of the people in the town took effect. This delayed him somewhat, as did also a rather stupid act on the part of the Spaniards. They had been ordered to sink the ships in the basin, but finding it impracticable, they blew up two of the Frigates and in so doing sank two English gun boats, which were near, killing a lieutenant and several seamen. Smith wrote to Hood:

Having now set fire to everything within our reach, exhausted our combustible preparations and our strength to such a degree that the men absolutely dropped on the oars, we directed our course to join the fleet running the gauntlet under a few ill directed shot from the forts Balgué and Aiguette.

Langara wrote:

In like manner were blown up two Frigates loaded with 4000 quintals of powder, on each of which a *chemin de souffre* was placed by the adjutant to the squadron Don Francisco Riquelme who acquired in that service the most distinguished honour, as did likewise the other two officers who were exposed during a considerable time to the fire of musquetry from the Insurgents belonging to the town.

On the morning of the 19th the Republicans entered Toulon. What the remaining inhabitants of the town had to expect, is well shown by what the *Representants* wrote the day preceding. Barras wrote:

*L'infâme Toulon est à nous rien ne peut le soutraire aux vengeances nationales. Demain le royaume de Louis XVII n'aura pas un pouce de terre.*[27]

Picord, Fréron and Robespierre *jeune* wrote *"demain nous serons dans Toulon occupés à venger la Republique"* [28]

The Republicans found a great deal of booty and many provisions in Toulon. These were increased each day by the ships which sailed in, thinking the city still in the hands of the Allies. The booty was gathered together, sold and the money divided among the soldiers. In the meantime the executions took place. In general it was a repetition of the punishment of Lyons; since thousands of the citizens left with the Allies, those who remained behind had to take their place, in spite of their remonstrances and declarations of republicanism.

The *Representants* wrote on Dec 20th[29]

*La vengeance nationale se deploie. L'on fusille à force. Déja tous les officiers de la marine sont exterminés. La Republique sera vengée d'une manière digne d'elle, les mânes des patriotes seront apaisées.*

As to the vessels which came in daily; *"Tout ce qui est etranger sur ses batiments est fait prisonnier tout ce que est français est fusillé"*. The *Representants* were in their element. Nowhere did they display their activity more than in "avenging the Republic". After about a week they seemed to have had enough. On January 5th they wrote:[30]

*Hercule, dit-on, eut plus de peine à nettoyerles etables d'Angias qu'à dompter les lions et les monstres. Pour nous nous preferons mille fois de nouvelles redoutes à attaquer plutôt que d'être condamnés à purger ce sol impur et grangrené. Nous se sommes entourés que de ruines, de supplices, de vengeances, de pleurs et de larmes que la rage du désespoire et non le repentir fait repandre.*

The enemies of Bonaparte, and of his name, have tried to connect him with these orgies of the *Representants*. In 1814 the Baron d'Imbert published in a pamphlet on the siege of Toulon, which was nothing more than a praise of himself and other *refugies*, together with a bid for the favour of Louis XVIII, the following letter as written by Bonaparte.

*Lettre de Bonaparte à la Convention. Citoyens Representants, C'est du champ de bataille, marchant dans le sang des traîtres que je vous*

---

27. Barras 18th Dec. R. A.
28. Letter 18th Dec. R. A.
29. *Recueil Aulard.*
30. *Recueil Aulard.*

*annonce avec joie que vos ordres sont exécutés, et que la France est*
*vengée. Ni l'âge, ni le sexe n'ont été épargnés: ceux qui avaient seule-*
*ment été blessés par le canon republican out été dépêchés par le Glaive*
*de la liberté et par la bayonette de l'égalité. Salut et admiration. Signé,*
*Bonaparte, citoyen sans-culottes.*

Others have said that of course Bonaparte must have taken part
in the massacres as the artillery was used to execute the people *"en
masse"*. They seemed to forget that there were 160 other artillery officers under him. The above letter is, it seems to me, most decidedly
a false one. Why should Bonaparte write to the Convention? Why
should he sign himself simply "Bonaparte" as if he were known to all
of them? Again had he, adopting the plan of the *Representants*, decided
to distinguish himself in this manner, he would surely have received
some mention from the *Representants*, at least from his friend Salicetti.
Further, there is absolutely no other indication that he was a party to
these executions. [31]

Like most of the officers, he propably looked upon them in a cold
half indifferent way, with some pity for the victims and much con-
tempt for the patriotic murderers. It must not be expected that Bonaparte, brought up in the atmosphere of the revolution, absorbed in his
own ambition, and looking on revolution as the means of satisfying
it, should regard such scenes with the same amount of human com-
passion as one would expect to find in a man today. A letter which
he wrote at this time,[32] seems to indicate that he looked upon such
measures as so much a matter of course, as not to mention them, one
way or the other; but that the first few days he spent in examining the
fortifications, and the naval and military stores of Toulon.

*Les Anglais n'ont fait que perfectionné et augmenté les fortifications de*
*la place, ainsi Toulon est plus dans le cas de se défendre aujourd'hui que*
*jamais . . . . . . Je m'occupe à faire construire les foures à réverbère. . . .*
*nous avons trouvé dans Toulon la même artillerie qui y etait avant leur*
*entrée, il nous reste encore 15 vaisseaux.*

These few lines indicate that he was occupied with quite different
things than "avenging the republic". The 15 vessels of which he spoke
formed part of those which took him later from this very port over
to Egypt.

---

31. The Duc de Raguse says in his *memoires* that Napoleon opposed this general
execution of the people.
32. *Correspondance de Napoléon.*

PART 2

DIPLOMATIC CORRESPONDENCE OF THE ALLIES
AND RESULTS OF THE FALL OF TOULON.

CHAPTER 1

# Declaration Published at Toulon

Toulon came into possession of the English so unexpectedly that Hood and others were quite unprepared with instructions relative to such an event. As Spain was much nearer, Langara received instructions early and the Spanish Court took such prompt measures as to procure them certain advantages which the English were afterwards unwilling to admit. Consequently there arose between these two powers disputes which lasted during the entire siege, and which were beginning to take dangerous proportions just as the fleets were forced to leave the harbour. Dundas wrote to O'Hara, Dec. 20:

> It must be remembered that from the manner in which Toulon came into His Majesty's possession it was impossible to be prepared with a force adequate to his wishes or to the importance of the acquisition.

And on the same day to Dundas:[1]

> You must be aware that Toulon came into our hands at a moment when it was impossible for us to have made any preparations for such an event.

That the English were not quite satisfied with Hood's declaration has been seen. At first the English Admiral, Goodall, was appointed governor of the town, and the Spanish admiral, Gravina, commander of the garrison. Hood wrote September 14:[2]

> We derive great assistance from Gravina who is the best sailor general imaginable; quick, intelligent, but not pretending to much military skill; and agreeing most cordially with the English.

1 Letters from Sec. Dundas to Lieut. Gen. Dundas 1793-4 British Museum Mss. Addit. 27,594.

2. St. Helens to Grenville Sept. 25. R. O.

The Spanish believed that the command of the troops was to remain in their hands. St. Helens wrote, September 25;[3]

> They (the Spanish troops) are to be accompanied by the *marechal de Camp* Don Rafael de Valdes (brother to the minister of the marine) who is to take the chief command of the troops on shore in the room of Admiral Gravina. I heartily wish that he may succeed equally well in maintaining a good understanding between the troops of the two nations.

The English however did not care to have their forces (including those of their allies) under the command of a Spanish general and resorted to underhanded methods to avoid it. General O'Hara was to be sent as governor to Toulon, and on September 21 he was appointed a lieutenant-general; which rank made him superior to the Spanish commander whom he must consequently supercede.[4] In the meantime the dispute broke out between Hood and Langara. Langara wrote to Hood October 19;[5]

> Notwithstanding that the king is very well satisfied with the good conduct of Rear-Admiral Gravina during the time that he has been commandant general of the combined troops at Toulon His Majesty, not to deprive the fleet of a general of his merit has resolved to relieve him from that command and that he should return to his ship to be employed in other important services, and has named Major-General Don Raphael Valdes to succeed him in the command. I communicate it to your Excellency for your due information and I hope that you will be pleased to give the necessary orders as I have done for his being, acknowledged.

Hood answered;

> I return to your Excellency a thousand thanks for your obliging communication of the arrival of Don Valdes to take upon him the command of his Catholic Majesty's troops in the room of our most esteemed friend Admiral Gravina and have not a doubt but the service of the common cause in which Spain and England are so very cordially united will as cordially be carried on. I beg to offer to your Excellency my sincere congratula-

---

3. Record Office.

4. Dundas to O'Hara Nov. 30 Dundas to Gen. Dundas Dec. 20. British Museum Mss.

5. St. Helens to Grenville No. 8 R. O.

tions that Admiral Gravina is going on so exceeding well.

It will be seen that the difference lay between Langara's "commandant general of the combined troops" and Hood's "the command of His Catholic Majesty's troops"; yet neither admiral approached the question directly.

A few days later however, Oct. 23, Langara informed Hood that Gravina had been promoted to the rank of lieutenant-general of the fleet and that the king had confirmed him[6] "the general command of the allied forces, in the possession of which he has been by the agreement between your Excellency and me".

Major-general Valdes was to command the Spanish troops. Hood no longer answered in an evading manner, but expressed himself so clearly as by no means to contribute to a good understanding between the admirals:

> No one can more sincerely rejoice than myself at my much esteemed friends promotion, but his Sardinian and Sicilian Majesty having been graciously pleased to confide their respective troops entirely to my disposal or to act under such British officer as I may judge fit to put them I am very much at a loss to conceive upon what ground Admiral Gravina can take upon him the title of commander in chief of the combined forces at Toulon; more especially as the town and its dependant forts were yielded up to the British alone and taken possession of by me. I shall therefore feel it my duty to put the Sardinian and Sicilian troops together with the British under the command of Major General O'Hara, the moment he arrives (who is now off the port) eventually subject to such orders as I may see fit to give.[7]

Then followed a long letter from each of the admirals; Langara declared that from the day they went on shore together, on Sept. 2, it was agreed that the command should be divided. Hood claimed that Toulon surrendered to him alone. This was true, as the English officers had been on shore and had arranged for the surrender before the arrival of the Spaniards; and the English fleet entered as soon as the Spanish was seen in the distance; Hood did not dare enter before. It was also true however that the Spaniards considered themselves on an equal footing with the English and had exerted themselves from the

---

6. Record Office. Letter published by Cottin.
7. Record Office. Published by Cottin.

beginning upon this understanding. St. Helens wrote to Grenville: [8]

In general though this Court certainly conceive themselves to be in strictness entitled to the nomination of the commander in chief of the forces on shore, in virtue of the agreement to that effect, which they suppose to have been concluded at the outset of the business between the two admirals, it seems to me that they are by no means disposed to insist pertinaciously upon that claim, being aware that it can hardly be considered as reasonable now that the Spanish troops in the garrison bear so small a proportion to those of Great Britain and her allies, but their feelings are of course very deeply wounded by those expressions in Lord Hood's letter to Admiral Langara on the 25th of October which so positively assert that the rights which have been acquired over the town and port of Toulon with its ships belong not to the two crowns jointly but solely and exclusively to Great Britain, contrary to the notions which have been hitherto entertained by this government, which they have so ostentatiously announced to their subjects and in consequence of which they have made such great and expensive efforts for the securing that important possession and I therefore cannot help taking the liberty of expressing a wish that their share in this joint right may at least nominally be preserved to them, since otherwise there is reason to fear that besides their withdrawing immediately from Toulon all their ships and land forces the effect of our late endeavours to cultivate a good understanding with them will be entirely lost and that they will cease to look towards England with any kind of cordiality or confidence.

This was his official report; the same day he wrote to Grenville: [9]

I am more anxious than I can express that for the reasons mentioned in my dispatch some means may be found for calming the very great degree of pique and ill-humour which this court have conceived on account of the Toulon business, by giving them at least nominally an equal share with us in the Possession or Trusteeship of that place and its appurtenances. It is certainly true that at the outset of the enterprise Admiral Langara had great reason to presume that it was upon that footing that he had been invited to concur in it: witness his joint proclama-

---

8. St. Helens to Grenville, Nov. 8. R. O.

9. *Idem.*

tion with Lord Hood, the ceremonies of the landing etc. Besides which even supposing that the motives which he and his court entertained upon that head were founded merely upon self delusion, we certainly were not ignorant that they acted from the impulse of that conception however erroneous, and therefore the deferring to undeceive them till the precise moment when their services were no longer needed would surely have an appearance, if not of ill-faith at least of Machiavelism, which would ill accord with the general character of the British Government. The Duke de la Alcudia seems to wish for some written agreement upon this subject but I imagine that that will hardly be found practical.

These two letters just given show that even the English ambassador at Madrid saw the justice of the Spanish claims. This dispute continued during the entire time of the occupation of Toulon, but before following it further it is necessary to speak of the Commission which was sent by the English to Toulon.

O'Hara had been appointed Governor of Toulon before the end of September; and Sir Gilbert Elliot, who was to have been governor of Dunkirk, was sent out also to take charge of the civil affairs. O'Hara and Elliot were to form with Hood a joint commission for the government of Toulon. Elliot left England the 11th of October, but it was not until the 22nd that Grenville, after consulting Pitt, informed the Court of Madrid, through St. Helens, of the appointment of this commission. [10] To settle on the spot such questions as may arise, His Majesty has;

> . . . .in execution of the trust undertaken in His name by Lord Hood authorized Sir Gilbert Elliot to proceed to Toulon to act conjointly with His Majesty's officers commanding his sea and land forces in the execution of a Commission respecting all the points of a Civil nature which may present themselves in the course of events at Toulon. His Majesty has also in consequence of the surrender of that place and from the sense of the necessity of relieving Admiral Goodall from the duties of a situation incompatible with the naval service, appointed Lieutenant-General O'Hara to succeed that officer as Governor of Toulon, and to take upon him the command of His Majesty's forces in that part of France. Lord Hood, Sir Gilbert Elliott and Gen-

---

10. Grenville to St. Helens Oct. 22. R. O.

65

eral O'Hara are severally directed to maintain the most cordial and confidential intercourse with the Persons employed by his Catholic Majesty, and to endeavour to the utmost to continue that good understanding which has hitherto prevailed there so much to the advantage of the common cause.

The foregoing was inserted in a letter to St. Helens on Pitt's advice. Pitt wrote October 17 to Grenville; [11]

We think there ought to be a sentence inserted distinctly mentioning that we have appointed a governor of Toulon in consequence of the place being surrendered to us; adding, of course, every proper assurance of our desire to cooperate with Spain in that question. We must take this line respecting Toulon whenever any question occurs between us and Spain on that subject.

Pitt foreseeing the possible objection of Spain added, "The sooner this step is taken, the more likely to avoid disgust".

Henry Dundas wrote to Grenville: [12]

It occurs to Mr. Pitt and to me that it is better not to keep back our having appointed a governor. The grounds on which we obtained possession, and the impossibility of Hood and the officers acting under him continuing to exercise the office and duties of Governor, are reasons too obvious for adopting the measure to be concealed.

Buckingham wrote to Grenville, asking about the division of command and added referring to the French ships at Toulon, [13]

. . . . it does not seem wise to risk the only safe deposit which the war has placed our hands.

The foregoing, as well as the tardiness in informing Madrid of the measures taken in London, shows that the English government was not dealing openly with Spain in reference to Toulon.

On Oct. 18 long and detailed instructions were sent to the English Commissioners at Toulon. The substance of these was as follows. [14]

The possession of Toulon and the prospect of its extensive consequences in the South of France have given occasion for the Commis-

---

11. Pitt to Grenville Oct. 17. Mss. of Fortesque.
12. Dundas to Grenville Oct. 20. Mss. of Fortesque.
13. Buckingham to Grenville Oct. 24th. Mss. Fortesque.
14. Record Office. Published almost in full by Cottin.

sion. It is to have three principal objects;

1st, to govern Toulon;

2nd, ("which is more extensive and more important") to induce other parts of France to have recourse to His Majesty's protection; to aid in the re-establishment of a regular government which is to end the internal disorders in France and open the way to a satisfactory termination of the war:

3rd., to take charge of any provinces or districts which should be occupied by His Majesty's arms or place themselves under his protection, "till some regular and general system shall have been re-established and a regular and a definite pacification concluded".

The Commission is also to publish immediately, and in His Majesty's name, a declaration addressed to the people of Toulon, "according to the tenor of the paper herewith transmitted". The powers of the other members of the commission must not interfere with the authority of the military governor in any matters of military detail.

As far as is consistent with this principle, due regulations ought to be framed for protecting as far as possible the persons of the inhabitants and for providing for the ordinary course of justice in civil affairs. The possibility of retaining the inhabitants in their civil and military employments must depend upon the dispositions they manifest and upon circumstances. The suffering of public meetings, or of authorizing and recognizing the deliberations of any committee must be governed by similar circumstances. A power must be exercised wherever it is necessary of confining, or sending away, suspected persons. "On all these points it is impossible to form specific instructions; the Commissioners will jointly exercise their discretion."

The second general head of instructions gives the following: His Majesty's primary object is to terminate the war as speedily as possible. Whatever may be the form of government in France His Majesty will feel himself entitled to demand such terms as may afford to himself and his allies reasonable indemnification for the past and security for the future. His Majesty is not disposed to prescribe any particular form, he is persuaded it is only on the foundation of hereditary monarchy (subject to such limitations as may be found advisable) that a rational prospect at present exists of any regular government being re-established.

All parts of France which may wish to deliver themselves from the tyranny of the present rule and concur in the restoration of a regular government, on the foundation of hereditary monarchy and accept His Majesty's protection, shall be well governed, and restored at the conclusion of a definite treaty of peace, "unless by the terms of such treaty it shall be agreed that any such place or district shall, for the purpose of indemnification or security be ceded to any of the powers who are engaged in concert with His Majesty in the present war. No idea is entertained of pushing that principle to the extent of proposing any plan of partition or dismemberment applicable to the interior of France; but it can only relate to such possessions on the frontiers as shall appear on fair discussion to come within the real objects which are professed. As this consideration is naturally more applicable to Austria than to any other continental power it does not appear that in the south of France, this exception can be material with respect to any district but such as may be contiguous to the frontier either of Spain or Sardinia, or possibly Switzerland, in case the Cantons may be brought to take an active part in the war".

No alarm is to be created from the idea of extensive projects of aggrandizement and dismemberment such as are not in His Majesty's contemplation. The declaration which you are to publish at Toulon will be circulated as speedily as possible in the interior of France. You will be particularly careful to state on all occasions His Majesty's conviction that the acknowledgement of a hereditary monarchy, affords the only probable ground for restoring regular government in France. His Majesty is far from meaning to pledge himself to any approbation of the articles of the Constitution of 1789 and is on the contrary persuaded that every part of the French nation which wishes for the re-establishment of Monarchy will ultimately see the impossibility of retaining many parts of that constitution, yet His Majesty has not felt this as any reason for withholding his protection from the people of Toulon, under the circumstances in which it was sought for.

Under the third head of instructions is found: all such places as choose to put themselves under the protection of His Majesty will be governed under His "general superintending power", but this authority must be subject to no fixed limitations, and must in time of war be inforced wherever it is necessary, by the military power. [15]

The Re-establishment of the former modes of Judicature, of the former Ecclesiastical establishment and particularly of the Provincial states in the provinces where they existed in a known

15. Following not published by Cottin.

and established form previous to the late troubles seem likely if they should be found practicable to be productive of great advantage and to lead to the restoration of order and good government. [16] But even in looking to these objects great caution will be necessary not to do violence to existing prejudices and it may be necessary unless the minds of the people at large should be disposed to such measures as I have stated, to postpone them for a time and to make no alteration in whatever may be the train and order of things which you may find existing father than is necessary for the fundamental object of acknowledging a monarchical government. [17]

The measures to be taken with respect to property which has been confiscated, and afterwards sold under the authority of the Convention, as well as that which may belong to persons who may continue in hostility to His Majesty; with respect to the circulation or suppression of *assignats*, and also with respect to the collection and appropriation of any public revenues, are also points of so much delicacy, and may depend so much on local circumstances, that it is not thought right, at present to make them the subject of positive instructions......

This *resumé* of the instructions sent to the commissioners at Toulon shows the ideas of Pitt, and the political views of the English at this time.

The declaration which was published at Toulon differed from that of Hood in two particulars:

1st; His Majesty was not willing to commit himself to the constitution of 1789, but simply regarded the reestablishment of an hereditary monarchy as the necessary form of stable government with which he hoped to make peace. He did not wish to specify any particular form nor to interfere with the internal affairs of France.

2nd; It was expressly stated that at the termination of a treaty of peace His Majesty expected for himself and his allies a just indemnification for the costs and dangers of a war which was forced upon him by France.

This declaration had been drawn up after a diplomatic correspond-

---

16. This proposal to re-establish the old provincial states as well as the idea that the people of the South of France would care very little what was taken on the frontiers or in the North shows that the new spirit which was awakened in the large majority of the French people was ill understood in London.
17. Following published by Cottin.

ence with the courts of Austria, Spain and Sardinia.

On Sept. 14 information was sent to Sir Morton Eden in Vienna that a public declaration would be made as to His Majesty's views on the war with France.

On Sept. 25 Eden wrote to Grenville:

. . . that Thugut had informed him that Austria agreed not to take any step toward the interior arrangement of France [18] without a previous and confidential communication with His Majesty. . . . . Sentiments entertained here were he (Thugut) added that France should be so far weakened as no longer to be dangerous. . . . . .On the subject of Indemnification the acquisition for Great Britain being to be looked for in the foreign settlements and Colonies of France, no jealousy, he observed, nor clash of interests could arise.

On Sept. 27 Grenville forwarded a draft of the proposed declaration to Eden. Speaking of the form of government in France; [19]

. . . . . it is infinitely better that this should be left to the feelings and experiences of the French nation itself than that Foreign Powers should seek to impose jupon that country particular points with respect to the modification of a monarchical government to which it may still be adverse. . . . .the claim for indemnification is no less carefully attended to. It appeared neither necessary nor advisable to specify particular objects of indemnification because these must of necessity depend on the events of the war. . . . . If on the whole the proposed declaration should meet with the concurrence of that Court it will be right for you to lose no time in returning the messenger in order that it may be published in His Majesty's name.

On Oct. 12 Eden sent off his answer in which he said that the Austrian minister agreed with the declaration but speaking of the indemnification wished [20]

. . . . that the expression '*telles que les Puissances Belligerantes ne peuyent se dispenser de demander*' might be omitted, as it might give a handle to all those who are engaged either actively or only apparently in the war, equally to bring forward claims of indemnification and increase the difficulties of the pacification. The King of Prussia would, he (Thugut) said, be the first

---

18. Record Office.
19,20. *Idem.*

to found on it pretensions for the further aggrandizement to which this court could never assent, till it has itself made acquitions equal to those of His Imperial Majesty in Poland.

In the place of these words he proposed to insert '*Sa Majeste ne peut se dispenser etc*'. I told him that I would transmit his observations for your Lordship's consideration though I could not agree with him in the propriety of the change proposed, as in a declaration of this kind the making no mention of the other Belligerent Powers might give them umbrage, might make them apprehensive of a separate peace without any attention to their interests and consequently render them less inclined to cooperate heartily towards the termination of the war.

The invitation to France to follow the example of the inhabitants of Toulon, he said he looked upon to be salutary as much as it regarded the towns situated at a distance from those parts to which His Imperial Majesty's views of indemnification were directed; but he trusted that should Lille or any other place contiguous to the Belgic provinces offer to surrender to His Majesty on the same conditions as Toulon that His Majesty would look upon himself as an auxiliary power on that side of France, and consider them as being to form the future barrier of those provinces, would accept them for the Emperor and to be governed in His name till the Peace.

This afternoon I waited again by appointment on M. de Thugut who delivered me a copy which I have the honour to inclose, of the Emperors proposed declaration. In reading over the paper I pointed out to him the words '*par les moyens que les lois fondamentales de sa constitution autorisent*'. I wished him to suppress them as they appeared to go beyond your Lordship's meaning and they might be construed to imply an intention to interfere in the internal arrangement of France and I particularly insisted on the advantage of a perfect union of sentiment on this important point of the declaration. He however adhered to these words as being more consistent with the form of government of His Imperial Majesty's Dominions—I spoke again to M. de Thugut on the subject of Prussia and Sardinia.

As to the former I had the satisfaction to find him disposed could the King of Prussia's effective cooperation for the conquest of Alsace and Loraine be absolutely secured to recommend to the Emperor to make a formal renunciation of any exchange whatsoever for Bavaria but in such a form as may save the Emperor's dignity. [21] He seemed however to have but little hopes of any effective support being procured from Prussia which opinion he considered as sufficiently justified by the events of the Campaign.

Offers of further assistance may he thinks be made, but he expects to find them clogged with such proposals of compensation as cannot be admitted in order that the refusal may be seized as a pretext to withdraw from the war. [22] He added that his expectation would be fully gratified if it could be possible to obtain from His Prussian Majesty His several contingents to the King, the Emperor and the Empire".

The foregoing gives one a further insight into the political relations at the time of the King's declaration. The English Court was anxious to act in consort with the Austrian in taking this step and had awaited her answer before publishing the declaration. It was not quite so particular about Spain. This is shown by the fact that the draft of the declaration was sent a week later to Lord St. Helens, and that his answer would not necessarily be waited for before publishing the declaration. This is another proof that England was less open to the Spanish Court than to the Austrian, even on the subject of Toulon where the two Courts were supposed to act in consort. The communication to St. Helens is dated October 4. It ran as follows: [23]

I transmit to your Excellency by His Majesty's command the draft of a declaration which His Majesty proposes to publish for the purpose of explaining to the well disposed part of the French nation His Majesty's views with respect to the prosecution of the present war. The circumstances of the late transaction at Toulon and the great probability that a similar disposition exists in many parts of France, have induced His Majesty to believe that the present moment is favourable for a declaration of this nature. It is uncertain whether the rapid succession of events by which the present crisis is marked may not render it expedient not to delay the publication of this paper till an answer can be received from the Spanish government respecting

---

21. It is interesting to see now under the influence of England Thugut is willing to modify his policy.

22. As early as 1793 Thugut seemed to have foreseen the possibility of a "Treaty of Basel."

23. Record Office.

its contents.

But even in that case His Majesty has felt that an early and confidential communication of it to the Court of Madrid was an attention on his part due to the union and friendship subsisting between the two crowns, and in case circumstances should admit of the delay, His Majesty will be extremely desirous of receiving from the Catholic King the fullest communication of His sentiments respecting it. His Majesty flatters himself that in all events the principles manifested in that declaration are such as will be found to correspond entirely with those of His Catholic Majesty. I feel it unnecessary for me to enter into any detailed discussion of these, as the paper itself will naturally suggest to your Excellency what is to be said upon it.

You will not fail to remark that in any intervention respecting the interior of France the King looks rather at the affording support to well disposed persons in that Kingdom than to the establishing there by external force any particular government. In recommending to the French to unite in the cause of monarchy His Majesty advises that only, which seems essentially necessary to the re-establishment of external or internal tranquillity, but carefully avoids discussing the various modifications and limitations of that form. His Majesty is persuaded that the entire re-establishment of an arbitrary Monarchy there, is neither practicable nor desirable.

His Majesty is on the other hand far from approving as an ultimate state of things the constitution accepted by the late King during the constraint which followed His being brought back from Varennes. But all the particular details of any intermediate system must as it appears be left to the discussion of the French themselves and foreign powers have no immediate object in looking farther than to the general principles stated in the inclosed draught. With respect to the principle of indemnification I have before stated to your Excellency that His Majesty in asserting His right on that subject as resulting from the unprovoked aggression of France admits in the most express manner the right of Spain founded on the same rule of equity and reason.

His Majesty even authorizes you to assure the court of Madrid of his sincere disposition to co-operate with that court as far as circumstances will permit in the attainment of such objects as

His Catholic Majesty may have in view for that purpose.

And His Majesty will receive with satisfaction and return with openness any confidence which the King of Spain may be disposed to place in His Majesty on that subject. Nothing could be more pleasing to His Majesty than to see the union and cordiality which has subsisted between the naval and military forces of the two Crowns on the occasion of the late event of Toulon.

His Majesty flatters himself that the result of that transaction must lead to establishing a still more intimate union between the two courts as well as among those who are respectively employed by them.—it is obviously to be desired that the combined forces of the powers engaged in the war against France should be enabled to profit of further openings and to make Toulon a centre of operations which may extend themselves as far as possible in the South of France where so much disposition exists to favour the cause of monarchy.

On Oct. 30 St Helens answered: [24]

Alcudia has acquainted me verbally that His Majesty's intended Declaration to the French Nation has been read by His Catholic Majesty with much satisfaction.

The Spanish were preparing a similar declaration. On Nov. 8 St. Helens wrote further that the declaration of Spain was quite satisfactory and corresponded with the English. As to the indemnification;[25]

Your Lordship will observe that the Duke de la Alcudia's letter admits and recognizes the justice of that claim in the fullest and most explicit terms so that a discussion of the details of that subject may now be brought forward whenever circumstances may render such a measure advisable.

The following is an extract from Alcudia's letter.[26]

With respect to the point of indemnity it appears to the King to be just that England should demand it for the expenses of the war which the French themselves have declared and His Majesty would contribute so far as he may be able to its being realized, at the same time that His Majesty claims the rights which in like manner belong to him upon the self-same ground, being well assured that both sovereigns will co-operate with mutual good faith in forwarding the just views which each of them

24-26. Record Office.

may propose to himself on the point in question.

Alcuda stated also that the Spanish King was quite satisfied with the declaration. On Nov. 30 Grenville wrote to St. Helens [27]

Monsieur del Campo having communicated to me the draughts of the proposed declaration to be published, by the court of Madrid I assured him in general terms of the King's approbation of that paper and your Excellency will not fail to express the same sentiments to the Duke of Alcudia. It has however not escaped the attention of this court that while in a letter written to you as well as in other communications between the two governments the principle of indemnity is not only recognized by the court of Madrid but it is even insisted upon as applicable to the situation of Spain no notice is taken of any views of this nature in the declaration which is to be addressed to the people of France.

Whatever may be the real views of Spain in this respect it seems very desirable that the Spanish Government should if possible be brought to enter into some explanation of this kind on that important and delicate point.—With respect to the indemnity of Spain, your Excellency will take an early opportunity to enter into some explanation with the Duke of Alcudia on this subject and you will endeavour to convey to him in a general manner such as may not excite jealously His Majesty's wish that in the result of the war the Spanish indemnity may be acquired on the frontier of France, by which means Spain would obtain a great and valuable accession of strength, particularly as to means of defence and would no longer be exposed to the invasion of France and continue thereby in some degree dependent on that country. Your Excellency's ability and experience will suggest to you the means of placing this proposal in its most favourable lights and of supporting it by the arguments the most likely to make impression.

In asking this explanation and in urging this proposal it will be proper that your Excellency should avow, on His Majesty's part, that the indemnity to this country can be found only in the French Possessions out of Europe, and you will therefore employ all your attention to convince the Spanish minister how little cause of jealousy to the Court of Spain arises from

---

27. *Idem.*

such acquisition, the immense territorial possessions of Spain in America are such as to furnish ample scope for the exertions of all the industry, capital and skill which Spain can employ and any acquisitions particularly in the Leeward Islands may truly be stated as being much less desirable to Her than to any other of the European Nations.

His Majesty conceives therefore and you will urge it as a proposal to the Spanish Ministers that both courts may with advantage further the views of each other in the points above mentioned. His Majesty by exerting His influence at the peace as far as circumstances will then admit, for procuring to Spain a valuable accession of territory on the frontier of France; and the Court of Spain by favouring in the like manner His Majesty's views of acquisition in the Leeward Islands.

With respect to St. Domingo it is conceived that the views of Spain may not unreasonably be turned to that quarter, and although the small advantage which Spain actually derives from the part of that island now in His possession might seem to afford a sufficient reason against Her looking to further acquisition there, yet it is probable that views of that sort are in fact entertained both by the hope of advantage and also as a means of deriving security against the dangers with which the Spanish colonies are menaced from the establishment of the principles on which the French have lately acted in the West Indies, and particularly in St. Domingo.

You will be aware that His Majesty's views also are in part directed towards that island, but it is by no means conceivable that these projects entertained by the two Courts are incompatible with each other. The extent of that island and the distance of the Spanish quarters from the parts nearest to Jamaica leaving full scope for arrangements being taken in concert respecting this island such as maybe mutually beneficial to both countries.

It is not the King's pleasure that you should actually propose any precise plan for this purpose or indeed any positive agreement with respect to the other objects of indemnification above mentioned, but it is judged to be extremely important for His Majesty's service that your Excellency should without delay enter into explanations on these points with the Spanish government, and endeavour to learn to what extent the Court of Madrid would be disposed to enter into engagements with His Majesty on the principles already laid down, and that you should transmit to me an account of the result of your conferences on this subject in order that a judgment may be formed of the best manner of bringing forward those discussions which the situation of Two Courts in the present moment seems to render indispensable.

In another letter of the same date Grenville wrote:

With respect to the political considerations with which this business is connected, I have in my other dispatch of this date stated to you at large the sentiments and views of His Majesty as to the general State of affairs, but I think it right in this place to give Your Excellency the fullest authority for entering into unreserved explanations with the Spanish Government on the subject of Toulon. His Majesty has in no case any view respecting that place different from that which has already been avowed in His name: That at the conclusion of peace that port should be restored to the Crown of France, and that in the interval it should serve in His Majesty's hands as a means of carrying on the war, and as a pledge of indemnity to Him and His allies, including in that description the crown of Spain whose claim to indemnity His Majesty has already distinctly avowed. [28]

Before its publication the declaration had also been communicated to the Sardinian Court, "as additional proof of confidence".

On November 20 the declaration was published at Toulon. Elliot wrote November 23. In regard to the ships [29] "the words '*ont été rendus*' appeared to give a little uneasiness to one or two members of the deputation as it conveyed something mortifying to their national spirit. I therefore substituted the word '*confiés*', which gave entire satisfaction and is at the same time consonant with the truth".

It is hoped that the foregoing extracts have given a clear idea of the circumstances under which this declaration arose. It may be regarded as the official statement of England's intentions in the beginning of the War of the First Coalition. As the fortunate termination of this war was regarded as near at hand, this declaration was to form a preliminary basis for the peace negotiations. Austria and Spain had agreed to it. It was not communicated to Prussia. It was Pitt who really framed

---

28. These lines state clearly England's intentions at Toulon.
29. Record Office. Commissioners to Toulon 1793. Hood, Elliot, O'Hara.

the declaration, and his idea was to treat with any kind of a stable government in France. Her internal affairs as long as she remained quiet were a minor consideration. The "indemnification" was the main object in London as also in Vienna and Madrid. On October 5 Pitt wrote to Grenville:[30] "We can treat with any form of regular government if it be solidly established".

Austria, however, was somewhat concerned as to the internal government of France, and it was out of consideration for her that England declared for hereditary monarchy. This difference in the drafts of the declaration had been noticed by Elliot, who wrote to Secretary Dundas on October 18:[31]

> The declaration as at last settled by you and Pitt differs from the last draft as to the following words, "*Quand la paix sera faite (et Sa Majesté declare par la presente qu'elle sera prête à la faire aussitôt qu'un gouvernement regulier sera établi en France)*". The words in the draft as last settled are "Whenever the Hereditary Monarchy of France shall be restored and a Treaty of Peace concluded.

The English Government has been reproached for not making this declaration agree entirely with the proclamation of Lord Hood, and with his understanding with the people of Toulon. In the first place, Hood acted without positive instructions, and more or less on his own responsibility; again, Toulon was not at that moment in a condition to give the people a right to expect England, or any nation, to accept their terms unconditionally. Hood might possibly have avoided the phrase "the Constitution of 89"; but the fact that he did not was not sufficient reason for the English to withdraw from the city, rather than commit themselves to a form of government which might have made a future peace impossible. England's object was to allow such latitude in this respect as to win over the greatest number of the inhabitants of France. "A stable form of government" was Pitt's idea, but it was finally agreed to insist upon "hereditary monarchy".

Although England had now come to a definite understanding with her allies Austria and Spain, there were still a number of questions pending between the different Courts; questions which excited jealousy and distrust, and thereby prevented combined action. Had the Allies put as much thought into their military operations as is found in their diplomatic negotiations, this vast scheme of indemnification might have been realized; but at Toulon, as elsewhere, the reckless

30. Mss. Fortesque.
31. Commissioners to Toulon.

Republican army, directed by a few men of genius, above all by Napoleon, proved more than equal to the disunited Allies. Three disputed questions preoccupied the courts at London and Madrid.

First, were the Spanish to be on an equality with the English in the Government of Toulon?

Second, what was to become of the French ships in case the Allies were forced to retire?

Third, were the brothers of the late King to be permitted to enter the city in an official capacity, or at all?

Finally, the question of the Austrian reinforcements, which were promised but failed to arrive, became a serious one between the courts of London and Vienna. The first stages of the dispute between England and Spain as to the command at Toulon have already been mentioned, and will be further spoken of in connection with the questions of the French princes, and of the fleet.

CHAPTER 2

# The Austrian Reinforcements

Quite early the English government received intimation that the French Princes wished to go to Toulon. On October 2 St. Helens wrote [1]

The Agents of the French Princes are extremely desirous to obtain permission for *Monsieur* to repair immediately to Toulon, and I am afraid that the Spanish Minister has given but too much encouragement to this idea although I have written to engage him to lay it aside, at least for the present.

On October 18 the Spanish Minister in London, Marquis del Campo, wrote to Grenville, and speaking of the affair of Toulon as a [2]

. . . .*nouveau chemin pour parvenir au grand but de calmer les troubles qui agitent et dechirent la France"*, and as *"ce grand point d'appui pour regenererla monarchie francaise"*, claimed that England and Spain *"se trouvent dans l'obligation de proportionner tout soutien et toute aide sinon à son captif monarque Louis XVII, au moins à celui qui se trouve à même de representer sa Personne".*—*"Les pretentious de l'Oncle du Roy doivent par consequent être regardées comme justes". "Il faut qu'il soit reconnu à Toulon en qualité de Regent de France. Ce Prince se trouvant sur le lieu—pourra agir d'une manière active, augmenter le parti du Roy, s'attirer les esprits encore vacillants et contribuer personelle et efficacement à voir realiser les intentions des Puissances.— Par ce moyen nos deux souverains auront la gloire d'avoir posé les premiers fondemens de la Paix dans le Royaume en établissant dans la dite ville le plus proche Parent de son monarque legitime: celui-ci benira éternellement les auteurs de son bonheur et les deux puissances alliés auront encore la satisfaction d'avoir triomphé par sa puissance et sa jus-*

---

1. Record Office.
2 Record Office. St. Helens' papers.

80

*tice de tous les efforts de l'iniquité.—C'est par les ordres express de ma*
*Cour que j'ai l'honneur de transmettre à V. Exce. ces considerations—*
*Le Roy mon maitre se flatte de trouver en elle (Sa M. Britannique) la*
*même manière de penser et les mêmes dispositions à soutenir Monsieur*
*dans Toulon, favorisant de toutes les manières possibles son établisse-*
*ment dans la dite ville, et ses progrès dans cette partie de la France.*

It may be readily seen that del Campo's arguments would not appeal to the English government. On October 22 Grenville wrote to
St. Helens:

It is by no means part of His Majesty's plan to exclude the late
King's brother from taking such share in the final arrangement
of that business (the internal affairs of France) as even in the
intermediate measures leading to it as their situation and events
which may arise in the interior of France may hereafter point
out. But when the circumstances which have attended the surrender of Toulon are taken into consideration it must surely be
felt that the admitting the French princes into that port is a step
leading to the most material and important consequences, and
which cannot be taken without mature deliberation.

His Majesty is by no means an advocate of the Constitution of
1789 and is on the contrary persuaded that no persons sincerely
wishing the restoration of Monarchy in France can ultimately
wish that it should rest on so precarious and insecure a footing.
But it must not be forgotten that the people of Toulon have
declared for monarchy as established by that Constitution, and
in consequence of that declaration put themselves under the
King's protection; that under that Constitution as finally settled,
the Comte de Provence has no absolute claim to the Regency
nor can the office of Lieutenant-General be conferred on the
Comte d'Artois.

And that in general the situation of the French princes and the
conduct, principles and supposed resentments of the persons by
whom they are surrounded cannot be considered as likely in
the present moment to conciliate the minds of the inhabitants
of that place. There is besides an essential and necessary condition before the King can consent to join His measures to those
of the French Princes to the degree that would be done by
admitting them into Toulon. It is indispensable that they should
enter into previous explanation respecting the principle of pacification and that they should recognize the justice of the claim

of His Majesty and His Allies, including the Catholic King to a fair indemnification for the *risques*, expenses and losses of a war commenced by the unjust aggression of France.

His Majesty by no means wishes the Court of Madrid to understand this communication as meant to operate as a final bar to the idea of employing the French Princes in France and particularly in the South. But His Majesty expects that no step towards this important determination should be taken, but in consort, and He thinks it absolutely necessary to ascertain beforehand, first whether the appearance of the Princes at Toulon would in fact be advantageous or prejudicial to the common interests in the present moment.

Secondly whether the Princes themselves are disposed to act reasonably and according to the exigencies of the moment relative to the interior of France; whether they and those who advise them are sensible of the necessity of laying aside animosities and resentments of waving inadmissible claims, and of submitting to be guided in their conduct by those powers whose support they ask, and lastly whether they are ready to enter into full and unequivocal explanation respecting the principles of indemnification above stated.

It is interesting to compare this communication, inspired by Pitt, with the foregoing sentimental note from Del Campo.

The English had taken prompt and decided measures to prevent the Spaniards from sharing their authority at Toulon, and they were naturally determined not to allow *Monsieur* to precede to that place as regent. On October 22, the same day as the foregoing communication was sent to Lord St. Helens, instructions[3] were forwarded to Francis Drake, (the English representative at Genoa, where *Monsieur* was supposed to go previous to embarking for Toulon,) to inform *Monsieur* of the impossibility of his proceeding to Toulon; of "the inconvenience which would result, both personally to that prince, and also to the general interests from any *éclat* taking place on this subject"; and also of the question of its being "agreeable to the inhabitants of Toulon".

Further if *Monsieur* insisted, Drake was to inform the Commissioners at Toulon that they were not authorized to permit him to enter without having first received instructions from His Majesty. . . . . "but you (Drake) will use every endeavour in your power by respectful and conciliatory representations, to prevent recourse being had to this ex-

3. Record Office. Published by Cottin.

tremity, and you will endeavour to persuade the ministers of the allied powers at Genoa to support you in these representations".

Meanwhile *Monsieur*, being in secret communication with Spain, took the matter into his own hands, and informed the English government through the Duc d'Harcourt, the representative of the Princes in London, of his decision to proceed to Toulon to assume the duties of regent. The English court was determined to prohibit him. On November 30 instructions [4] were sent to the Commissioners at Toulon not to admit him. On the same day orders were hurried to John Trevor in Turin to stop *Monsieur* as he passed through the city: to say to His Sardinian Majesty that it is impossible for *Monsieur* to go there without the approbation of the King of Great Britain. [5]

If *Monsieur* should have already quitted Turin previous to your receiving this despatch you will urge the King of Sardinia to send after him some proper person for the purpose of making these representations both in the King's name and in that of the King of Sardinia and in order if possible to prevent the *éclat* which must arise from *Monsieurs* persisting in His project and being exposed to a public refusal on the part of His Majesty's officers at Toulon.

Long and precise instructions were sent to St. Helens, by Grenville, on November 30. [6]

With respect to the great question of a recognition of the authority of *Monsieur* as Regent, it seems to depend in a great degree upon the result of discussions of the nature already mentioned and also upon the course of events to which the war may give rise. His Majesty is by no means adverse to this recognition but in order that it should be rendered advantageous to the common cause it must be combined both with circumstances in the interior of France favourable to it, and also with such explanations on the part of the princes as may shew that their views are not in opposition to those of the principal Powers of Europe, whose aid they seek, and that they are willing rather to listen to the advice of those Powers and to yield to the necessity of the existing circumstances than to give scope to the passions and prejudices of those by whom they are surrounded.

Soon after the note on this subject was presented to me by

4. Commissioners to Toulon. Record Office.
5. Foreign Office, Sardinia. Record Office.
6. Record Office.

Monsieur Del Campo an application was received from the Comte d'Artois praying His Majesty's assistance to transport himself into Brittany, and to maintain himself there. The answer . . . was favourable, though not conclusive. We expressing an inclination on His Majesty's part to comply with the request, but stating the necessity of previous explanation You will communicate these particulars to the Court of Madrid as forming the answer to the proposal made by that Government on the subject of *Monsieur*, and as manifesting the King's disposition to concur with His Catholic Majesty by every means in His Power for the promotion of those salutary objects which the two courts have in view.

In another letter of the same date Grenville wrote: [7]

In addition to what I have already written to your Excellency on the subject of Toulon I am now to mention a circumstance respecting that place which His Majesty has seen with much concern. A letter for His Majesty from the Comte de Provence was yesterday delivered to me by the Duke d'Harcourt. By the copy which I enclose to your Excellency of this letter you will see that in it, the Comte de Provence announces to the King, as a resolution already taken, His design of going to Toulon, and that he takes upon himself to say that he goes there to exercise the functions of Regent, and I am informed that he is actually set out upon this journey.

If no other considerations had prevailed, the respect due to His Majesty required that no steps should be taken by *Monsieur* with regard to Toulon, without first submitting it to His Majesty's consideration and decision. The question whether the Comte de Provence should go there at all, in the present moment, is one worthy of much deliberation. His going there as regent, while the place is in its present situation, is liable to still more question; but attempting to take these steps without the King's previous consent while the port and town of Toulon are held by His Majesty and occupied by his forces, cannot in any manner be permitted

It is proper that I should not conceal from your Excellency the suspicion entertained here that this step has been secretly suggested or at least encouraged by the Court of Spain, as one, the

---

7. *Idem.*

success of which would tend to increase their influence in Toulon. The possibility of this only increases the necessity of your holding a firm and decided language both as to the absolute command to be exercised at Toulon by Governor O'Hara, as also to this particular point of *Monsieur's* admission there.

Information having been, sometime since, received which seemed to make it not improbable that *Monsieur* would take the step, which he has now announced, provisional orders were put to His Majesty's officers at Toulon directing them not to admit of *Monsieur's* coming there, without His Majesty's previous consent being signified to them, and measures were taken to prevent the *éclat* which a public demand and refusal on this subject might produce, by previously apprising *Monsieur* of the embarrassment to which such an event would expose him.

I have now taken further steps for this purpose, but as they may fail in their effect I have received the King's orders expressly to instruct your Excellency to represent, in the strongest terms, to the Spanish government the disrespectful conduct of *Monsieur* toward His Majesty on this occasion, and to announce to them the orders which His Majesty has thought proper in consequence of it, to send to Gov. O'Hara positively prohibiting him from suffering *Monsieur* to enter Toulon. In your communication on this subject you will not appear to believe that the Spanish government could be in any way a party to this inconsiderate and improper step on the part of *Monsieur*.

But you will remark that this instance of disrespect towards the King obliges him to suspend the discussions which he had been willing to open with *Monsieur*, respecting the recognition of His claim to the Regency of France, according to the desire which had been expressed by the Court of Madrid. You may however add that His Majesty on being informed that *Monsieur* has abandoned his present project and is sensible of the impropriety of his conduct towards His Majesty, will be ready to resume the consideration of that point on the grounds which I have stated to you at large in my other letter of this day.

Before this time the agents of the princes were active in Toulon also, and apparently in understanding with the Spaniards. On Nov. 23 the *Comité de Surveillance* and the sections of Toulon announced to Elliot their desire for the restoration of the ancient form of government, for the acknowledgment of *Monsieur* as Regent, and for the immediate exercise of his authority in Toulon. I shall give here the original reports relating to this question. The first is a letter from Elliot to Henry Dundas;[8] dated Toulon Nov. 24.—

> I have received the enclosed paper from the *Comité de Surveillance* and the sections of Toulon, by which you will see how decided the public mind is at Toulon for the restoration of their ancient government. The warmth with which they desire the acknowledgment of the Regent and the immediate exercise of his authority here, without touching at all on the constitution of 1789, confirms extremely the idea I had formed of their dispositions. It is worthy of remark that the sections are the most popular assemblies that can be conceived, being composed without distinction of all inhabitants who think proper to attend them. I confess that every view I have on the subject inclines me strongly to think that the acknowledgment of the Regent by all the combined Powers is a measure highly desirable.
>
> The interests of the monarchy which (though His Majesty is not ultimately pledged to that principle) we have in the meanwhile avowedly espoused, and the restoration of which, is infinitely the most important object of the war, would surely be much promoted by the advantage of an ostensible and legitimate representation of the royal authority. I am persuaded it would detach from us no support on which we can depend, and it would add a greater accession of numbers and zeal to the service. It is a measure so likely to work on the imagination of Frenchmen that one cannot help considering it as at least possible, that a general and sudden turn might be given to the affairs of France by this single change in our system.
>
> I am aware that other objects may justly, and perhaps must in point of policy, as well as of fidelity to our allies, be taken into the consideration of this subject and that on these accounts, this resolution cannot be adopted otherwise than in consequence of a previous discussion with the princes, and by a general concert with the combined Powers. I am therefore glad to hear that the first steps seem to have been taken, and considering that one of our allies, the court of Spain, has already declared its sentiments, I flatter myself with the hope of the negotiation being brought to an early and favourable conclusion—the more I learn of the

8. Record Office.

true nature of the counter-revolutionary spirit in France, the more I am inclined to the opinion, I have taken the liberty of delivering, and the more essential I think it to our success that the measure should be adopted.

With regard to the application made to me by the sections of Toulon on this subject, I shall be able to prevent their carrying any measure into execution until I have the honour of receiving His Majesty's commands. I cannot say that I see any local inconvenience in the admission of the Regent into Toulon, and the establishment of his authority here, and it might possibly produce a good effect in the adjacent country, and even in the besieging army, at the same time it must be observed that by such a condescension His Majesty would perform his engagements for the redelivery of Toulon earlier than can be claimed by the terms of the convention: and possibly some advantage might be lost in treating for the terms of peace.

But if anything were gained by it, towards accelerating the settlement of France, I confess, I should think all disadvantages on other points sufficiently compensated. There is too much reason to fear that Austria is more indifferent to the main object of the war, and more attached to points of her own, than she professes to be. Prussia we know is not to be depended on, and if Great Britain does not throw her whole weight into the scale of a more enlarged and sounder policy, there is great reason to fear for the issue of this contest.

Elliot enclosed the following:

ANSWER OF THE COMMISSIONERS AT TOULON TO THE

COMITÉ DE SURVEILLANCE RESPECTING THE REGENT. [9] 27TH OF NOV.

*Nous avons reçu avec beaucoup d'interet la communication qui nous a été faite de vos deliberations et de celles des sections de Toulon, relativement à la Regence. Nous y reconnaissons avec le plus grand plaisir des sentiments dignes à la fois du patriotisme et de la sagesse de cette ville respectable. Nous partageons avec elle non seulement le désir de voir renaître l'ordre sous un gouvernment fondé sur des bons principes, non seulement les sentiments de loyauté et d'attachment pour votre jeune et infortuné monarche, mais aussi ceux du respect et de la vénération, pour la famille de vos rois, et surtout pour l'auguste personnage qui est l'object de vos veux.*

9. Record Office.

*Nous nous trouvons néanmoins dans l'impossibilité de concourir immé-*
*diatement à l'accomplissement de vous souhaits et nous désirons vous*
*faire part des obstacles qui s'y opposent. La Regence de la France inter-*
*esse l'Europe entière et surtout les Puissances coalisées, puisque dans le*
*circonstances actuelles l'autorité du Regent comme celle du trône même*
*ne peut être réalisée que par leur sécours et par des efforts immense de*
*leur part. Cet object donc doit de toute nécessité, comme par toutes les*
*obligations tante de la saine politique que des sentiments honnêtes (les*
*seuls qui puissent animer ces Princes illustres) être traité directement*
*avec les cours qui combattent les ennemis de votre Roy.*

*Une affaire aussi importante et qui embrasse des rélations politiques*
*aussi étendues et aussi combinées ne peut être terminée avec effet ni*
*peutêtre même tentée avec avantage par une seule ville respectable à la*
*verite à toutes sortes de titres, mais pour le moment non seulement iso-*
*lée du reste de la France, mais ayant contracté pour l'interet du royaume,*
*comme pour son propre salut, des rélations récentes et sacrées avec une*
*autre puissance. Il est evident dans tous les cas que les ministres de sa*
*Majesté Britannique doivent être absolument incompetens à décider*
*sur ces objets sans avoir specialement consulté leur cour et obtenu des*
*pouvoirs directs. Tout ce qu' ils pourront faire pour seconder le zéle*
*louable des habitans de Toulon, est de soumettre sans delai cette matière*
*interessante à la sagesse et aux lumières de Sa Majesté et d'attendre*
*ses ordres.*

*Jusqu'alors ne nous trouvant point autorisés à compromettre Sa Majesté*
*sur la question de la Regence, nous pouvons encore moins consentir à,*
*la proposition qui a été faite d'appeller Monsieur le Comte de Provence*
*à Toulon, pour y exercer les fonctions de Regent parce que ce serait des-*
*tituer Sa Majesté Britannique avant l'epoque stipulé de l'autorité qui*
*lui a été dernièrement confinée à Toulon. Ces raisons ne nous obligent*
*cependant point de nous opposer au desir que pourraient avoir les habit-*
*ans de cette ville de parter leurs hommages aux pieds de ce Prince et de*
*lui exprimer tous les voeux que doivent inspirer ses vertus personelles*
*ou que peuvent réclamer les droits de sa naissance.*

   *A Toulon ce 27 de Novembre 1793.*
   *Signé; Hood, Elliot, O'Hara.*

Elliot commented on this answer in another letter to Henry Dundas, on the same day:

We have endeavoured to conform ourselves to the spirit of His
Majesty's commands as conveyed in your despatch of the 22

of October. . . But although we have been careful not to commit His Majesty on the question and have positively refused to admit the princes into Toulon, without His Majesty's orders we did not think it necessary to prevent the inhabitants from paying to him any compliment they thought fit, or acknowledging in their own name his right to the Regency. We thought it might even be advantageous that they should execute that part of their intentions because in the first place it will unite great numbers of them in a measure in which the constitution of 1789 is not mentioned, and in the next place, will afford security for their steadiness, as it renders their case more desperate with the convention.[10]

The retreat of the Allies from Toulon brought this question to an end. The English whose main object in the war was the "indemnification" regarded a stable form of government as the necessary condition for the obtaining, as well as for the peaceful enjoyment of, this indemnification. Toulon they intended to hold as security for it. The interests of the French monarchy for which England had declared principally out of consideration for Austria, and perhaps for her other Allies, were not thought of as sufficiently important to justify her sacrificing her authority at Toulon by the admission of *Monsieur*. Again, the French fleet was to be considered.

Although nowhere mentioned, it is certain that the English were conscious of the fact that by the admission of *Monsieur*, the ships also would be under his command and consequently neither come into English hands nor even be destroyed. The removal of the fleet formed part of England's plan for supremacy in the Mediterranean. Spain, however, beside her natural inclination to aid the French princes from dynastic interests, was not at all adverse to the idea of the English authority at Toulon being superseded, more especially as her own influence would be far greater with the Regent than with the English. The Sardinian Court to which the princes had also applied, was at this time quite subject to the interests of England.

Neither from Hood's declaration which recognized the constitution of 89, nor from the King's declaration which declared for hereditary monarchy, was England under any binding moral obligation to recognize *Monsieur* as Regent. As a political move it is hard to say what would have been the result. In all probability *Monsieur* would

---

10. These three communications just given are all from the Record Office.

have arrived too late to have had any material influence upon the affairs of Toulon.

The dispute as to the division of authority always remained an unsettled one. In the beginning of November St. Helens advised Alcudia to wait until he (St. Helens) received news from England and meanwhile that both generals should command. On November 8 St. Helens wrote to Grenville:[12]

> The Duke de la Alcudia has nominated M. Ocarez (who was *chargé d'affaires* in France, at the time of the death of the late King) to reside at Toulon as Plenipotentiary from this court; an appointment which seems to have been created in imitation of that of Sir Gilbert Elliot, however I do not find that he is invested with any similar Commission, his instructions being merely to correspond regularly with the department of the first secretary of State.

On November 13. St. Helens wrote further:[13] that the dispute between the admirals continued, but that Hood assured him that it would not interfere with the cause, "O'Hara and Gravina waving entirely the question relative to the chief command:" on November 27, that the differences were arranged and that O'Hara was to have the chief command of the combined forces on shore and Gravina the government of the city. Hood however was not in a very conciliatory mood especially as he had a very low opinion of the Spanish. As early as October 11 he wrote to Trevor [14] "I must mention to you in confidence that no dependence can be placed in the Spanish or Neopolitians, they cannot be left anywhere to themselves."

On November 20 Elliot wrote to St. Helens, complaining of the quality of the Spanish soldiers; [15]

> It is his (O'Hara's) opinion, and I believe Lord Hood's, that if you can by any means obtain better troops, or if not, if you can even withdraw those that are here you will render a service to the garrison If any disaster should take place here it will become a very serious question, in what manner the French ships should be disposed of. In that event if Spain in pursuance of their present notions of *equality* should set up any claim of participation in the possession of those ships our measures will be

12. Record Office.
13. Record Office.
14. Foreign Office. Sardinia 1793. R. O.
15. Commissioners to Toulon 1793. R. O.

exposed to great embarrassment. I need say no more to satisfy your Lordship of the importance of this matter and we leave it with great confidence in your hands.

This shows conclusively that even Elliot, who falsely regarded the restoration of monarchy as the principal object of the war, and who was in favour of recognizing *Monsieur* as Regent, had no intention of admitting any "equality", in fact any share, in the distribution of the French ships. In such a state of affairs a more serious turn in the old dispute seemed inevitable; but the position of the Allies having become gradually quite precarious, the political questions fell into the background. Even before November 30, the English more than doubted the strength of their hold on the town.

On Nov. 23 Elliot wrote to Dundas;[16]

It seems to me that the possession of this place is precarious, and that every day is critical": the next day to Lady Elliot, "O'Hara thinks as ill as possible of this business as it now stands; but re-inforcements may be expected before the worst may happen. Lord Hood is over confident and will never admit the slightest doubt of our keeping the place.[17]

The English had changed their opinion on another question also. On Oct 19. Mulgrave wrote to Trevor[18]

You must not send us one *emigré* of any sort; they would be a nuisance, they are all so various and so violent in their prin-ciples of *gouvernment* whether for despotism, Constitution or Republic, that we should be distracted with their quarrels and they are so assuming, forward, dictatorial and full of complaints, that no business could go on with them. Lord Hood is adverse to receiving any of them. You must therefore put them off as civilly as you can.

A little more than a month later Elliot informed Dundas [19] that they had sent to Italy for twenty to eighty emigrant officers, and on December 8, [20] Hood, Elliot and Dundas informed the emigrants that they might serve under their own officers, but subject to the Govern-ment of Toulon. Not many were to serve as officers, but principally as

16. Commissioners to Toulon. R. O.
17. *Life of Elliot*, Minto.
18. Sardinia, Foreign Office. R. O.
19. Letter Nov. 27th. Commissioners to Toulon.
20. Elliot to Trevor. Dec. 8. Foreign Office. Sardinia. R. O.

private soldiers which "*l'amour de la Patrie sçait concilier avec l'honneur de la noblesse Française*". They were also directed to ask the approbation of the princes as that would help the cause.

On Dec. 18. Trevor wrote to Grenville, [21]

The emigrants wait for His Royal Highness orders before they determine upon accepting our offers of receiving them at Toulon. I cannot doubt but that he will tell them to go.

The emigrants were still negotiating in Switzerland when Bonaparte's batteries had driven the Allies from Toulon.

On Dec. 1. Elliot wrote to Dundas:[22]

Nothing very important has occurred in the political affairs of this place and indeed that department is naturally rather in the background, while our situation is so critical.

This marks the end of the dispute between the two nations in the city itself. Other thoughts occupy their attention. Elliot wrote Dec. 9.[23]

I consider our possession of this place very precarious, which is not surprising, considering that I have heard that opinion from every military man of rank since I came here.

On Dec. 12 "General Dundas is in very low spirits and seems to despond more than ever". The tone of the two courts, especially of the Spanish, was far from being conciliatory. The two following communications show that the disputed question bade fair to become insoluble. The fall of Toulon rendered a solution unnecessary.

Grenville to St. Helens. Whitehall. Dec. 1.

The original tenor as well as the particular expressions of Monsieur Del Campo's late notes, are so entirely inconsistent with the *relacions* in which the two courts have been placed with respect to each other by the late negotiations and by the circumstances which still exist that it is thought absolutely necessary that Your Excellency should ascertain whether the form and language of those notes were prescribed to him by his court, or whether they arise solely from ill disposition towards this country of which he has given such repeated proofs. And if the latter should be found to be the case Your Excellency will no

---

21. Foreign Office. Sardinia. R. O.
22. Commissioners to Toulon. R. O.
23. To Lady Elliot. *Life of Elliot*. Minto.

doubt judge it absolutely necessary to adopt some proper expedient by which the Duke of Alcudia may be apprised how little Monsieur Del Campo's conduct appears calculated to promote union and good understanding between the two countries.

St. Helens wrote to Grenville on Dec. 25.

But at any rate I think it my duty to acquaint your Lordship without loss of time, that this court does not hitherto appear to be disposed to relinquish voluntarily their pretended right to the perpetual nomination of the commander in chief of the combined forces in Toulon unless it be on the evidently inadmissible condition, of their being allowed to remove from that port and to retain under their sole custody, the greater part, if not the whole, of the French fleet now lying there: . . . . and that they have also rendered the arrangement of this disputed point still more difficult than before by nominating to the command of the Spanish troops at Toulon the celebrated Count O'Reilly who (not to mention the objections that might be stated against his personal character and dispositions) is a Lieutenant General of near 30 years standing and consequently superior in point of seniority to any officer of that rank in the British Army.

One other question which preoccupied the British cabinet during the entire siege was, that of the Austrian reinforcements. In the *rapprochement* between London and Vienna which came about in the War of the First Coalition, and which had by the publication of the King's Declaration taken the form of an explicit policy of "indemnification", the English court had expected the assistance of from 12,000 to 15,000 Austrian troops for any offensive operations which might take place from the Mediterranean. On hearing of the surrender of Toulon, Pitt wrote to Grenville telling him to press the Emperor to send troops, and on Sep. 14 such instructions were sent to Eden.

As early as Sep. 11 Eden informed Grenville [24] that he had demanded troops from Thugut, who made excuses saying that they were needed on the Rhine, and complaining of the backwardness of Prussia. On Sept. 25 Eden wrote that he urged that a force should be sent to Toulon and Thugut replied that he would recommend it to His Majesty. But at the same time Eden wrote to Trevor telling him that the troops were coming; as if it had been already settled. Austria did promise the troops however, but under conditions.

---

24. Austria. Sir Morton Eden. Record Office.

Eden wrote to Auckland: [25]

> This country gives *us* 5000 men . . . but will not allow them
> to be employed offensively to make conquests for the King of
> Sardinia unless that Sovereign will (if any are made) yield them,
> though in a very inferior proportion something in return for
> the share of this court in the Novarese.

Thaon de Revel says in his *Memoirs*;

> *Les troupes Autrichiennes qui étaient dans les garnisons de l'état de
> Milan y étaient restées paisiblement an lieu de marcher sur Lyon,ce
> qui en eut empêché la chute et porté un coup mortel à la revolution.
> L'Angleterre demandait que les Autrichiens reunis aux Piedmontais
> chassassent les Français du comté de Nice d'une partie de la Provence
> et que l'on entr'ouvrit une communication directe et sure avec Toulon.
> L'apprehension de la Cour de Vienne que le Roi de Sardaigne n'eut
> des succès, s'opposa dans cette occasion comme dans toutes les autres
> a tout ce que le lien commun de la coalition conseillait si fortement.
> Elle espérait que si le Roi de Sardaigne se trouvait dans l'embarras il
> consentirait à lui ceder une partie des acquisitions faites anciennement
> sur l'état de Milan.*

This jealousy of Sardinia, a distrust of England and a failing to see
any tangible and immediate gain were the real reasons why Austria did
not send the troops. The reasons she put forward were others. [26] On
Oct. 30 Eden wrote: [27]

> In a conversation with the Austrian minister he repeated with
> some appearance of alarm the danger of their present situa-
> tion unsupported by Prussia and the Dutch and their num-
> bers reduced by repeated losses, particularly in the affair before
> Maubeuge, and asked me if in the case Toulon should be found
> from the reinforcements already arrived there not to stand in
> need of the troops promised from hence.

The troops were looked for at Toulon and Hood dispatched Admiral Goodal to Genoa to bring them but the ships returned as empty
as the departed. Finally however the English Cabinet, impatient at this
delay, assumed more and more express terms in demanding the troops,

---

25. *Correspondence of Auckland.*

26. On Nov. 4. Thugut received information from London "*assez propre à calmer nos
inquiétudes sur les intentions des Anglais relativement à Dunkerque.*" *Vertrauliche Briefe von
Thugut. von Vivenot.*

27. Eden to Grenville R. O.

as the following instructions to Eden will show. They are dated Nov. 11. [28]

> You will remonstrate in the strongest terms against this delay as a positive breach of faith and as likely to be in its consequences highly injurious to the common interests. . . .

Nov. 24. [29]

> You will therefore now admit of no further excuse but formally claim the immediate execution of the engagement and lose no time in apprizing me of the result.

On Dec. 8 Eden replied: [30]

> I called on Thugut . . . . and in obedience to your Lordship's express directions demanded, in His Majesty's name, an order for the immediate march of the reinforcements promised to His Majesty for the support of Toulon.

It was not until Dec. 16. that Eden was finally able to assure John Trevor that[31] "every difficulty is removed" and "that His Imperial Majesty has issued his orders for the immediate march of the troops for Toulon." This time the Austrians were undoubtedly sincere but as is seen, it was too late. Before this note could reach Trevor, Toulon was lost. The English had been over-confident at Toulon. Although Dundas, the secretary of war, had been repeatedly warned, he could not realize that it was possible to lose the place. He counted too much on the bad quality of the Republicans. As late as Dec. 27. troops were being embarked at Cork for Toulon, [32] and but a few days before Paymaster General Lennox was sent from London. [33]

28,29, 30. Record Office.
31. *Letters from Dundas*. British Museum. Mss. Additional 27, 594.
32. *War Office Letter Books*. Commander-in-chief. (1792-94) R. O.
33. *Admiralty Records*, War Office. (1782-1794). Dec. 20. R. O.

CHAPTER 3

# Role of Bonaparte

The news of the fall of Toulon caused in republican France and especially in Paris, the wildest joy. On Dec. 24. it was announced by Barrère in the Convention. At the same time he made a motion that *"L'armée dirigée contre Toulon a bien mérité de la Patrie."* The entire assembly arose with loud shouts of approbation. A few days later Robespierre began one of his long speeches with, *"laissons l'Europe et l'histoire vanter les miracles de Toulon et préparons de nouveaux triomphes à la liberté"*. The Convention decided to declare a general holiday and on Dec. 30. the great *"fête de rejouissance"* took place. David was ordered to prepare it.

The entire Convention took part in the tremendous procession. For weeks the *theaters* gave popular performances *"en rejouissence de la reprise de Toulon,"* and *"La prise de Toulon"* was often read in the papers of that time as the title to a play which was supposed to win popular favour. Not only in Paris and in France, but even in America and in Constantinople one celebrated the fall of Toulon. As to the reception of the news in Spain, St. Helens wrote on January 8. [1]

> With regard to the sensations produced here by the late abandonment of Toulon it seems to me that if this court feel any concern on that account it arises rather from certain collateral considerations than from their conceiving that event to be in itself prejudicial to the common interests they are of the opinion that by the destruction of the arsenal and shipping of Toulon we have secured all the essential advantages which the surrender of that place was ever likely to have afforded without the burthen and risk of maintaining possession of it, this seems

---

1 Record Office. 2192-7

to be likewise the opinion of the public at large.

Lord St. Helen's opinion was corroborated by the *Gazetta de Madrid* which gave the accounts of the evacuation. But from now on, an enmity gradually developed between England and Spain, and in the Declaration of War by Spain in 1796 is found the following passage:

This ill faith became manifest in the most critical moment of the 1st. *Campagne.*from the manner in which Lord Hood treated my fleet at Toulon where he attended to nothing but the destruction of what he could not carry away with him.

As the Spaniards were by no means an inactive party to the destruction referred to, this passage is open to some criticism; but it shows none the less that the differences between the English and Spanish left some impression. Later on it was even stated openly in London that the Spanish blew up the ships in the harbour of Toulon purposely to destroy the English boats. This statement is no doubt false, but it shows to what extent the ill feeling between the two countries went.

In England the news was received with surprise but with no great amount of disappointment. The Opposition welcomed it however as they hoped to use it against the government. Nelson's opinion was in general the most prevalent one. [2]

For England the getting rid of such a place is a most happy event. Our money would have gone very fast. The quitting of Toulon by us I am satisfied is a national benefit.

The Earl of Elgin wrote to Grenville on the [3] "unfortunate news" but added "the destroying the fleet and arsenal and saving the garrison are great palliatives". At the opening of Parliament on Jan. 21, 1794. the following reference is made to Toulon, in the King's speech:

. . . .the temporary possession of the town and post of Toulon has greatly distressed the operations of my enemies; and in the circumstances attending the evacuation of that place an important and decisive blow has been given to their naval power, by the distinguished conduct, abilities and spirit of my commanders, officers and forces both by sea and by land.

This was to a great extent the opinion in official circles. Lord Star in the address of thanks replied:

Since the memorable Battle of La Hogue a more brilliant en-

---

2. *Nelson's Dispatches.*
3. Elgin to Grenville. Dec. 29. Fortesque Mss. 4

terprise had not been achieved than that at Toulon by Lord Hood. The destruction of the Arsenal and naval stores of the second seaport of France was a circumstance that she could not repair for years. It must necessarily cripple her navy for the present and for years to come and. prove the most fatal blow that was struck at the French marine.

The Opposition in Parliament however used the affair at Toulon as an opportunity of condemning the conduct as well as the object of the war. Fox was especially bitter in his criticism, while Pitt defended the government. On the opening of the session in Jan. 94. in his attack upon the government Fox referred frequently to Toulon. "When we have been driven from Toulon in a manner so afflicting if not disgraceful".... He then pointed out the difference between the object of gaining;

> .....some solid advantage for ourselves, as an indemnification for the expenses of the war and that of giving such a government to France as ministers might think it safe to treat with. ... Toulon was taken by the British in consequence of certain conditions stipulated by the inhabitants. And yet even with the certainty of the guillotine before them these inhabitants were so unwilling to assist the British, that no other than an ignominious evacuation could be effected. If it was right so to take it, it became a matter of indispensible duty to defend it. Toulon, purchased by compromise you have lost with disgrace; you have placed yourselves in a point of view entirely new to British character, you have proved yourselves neither useful as friends, nor respectable as enemies.

On May 30. in speaking of the King's declaration he said;

> A declaration in the name of his majesty afterwards came out different indeed from this: verbose, obscure and equivocal like the production of men who are afraid of saying anything distinctly, who wish not their meaning to be clearly understood: that stript of all the elegant rubbish with which it was loaded declared only this, that the restoration of monarchy without specifying what kind, was the only condition upon which we could treat with France.

Pitt replied;

> .... the right honourable gentleman proceeded to bring for-

ward a charge of inconsistency from the declaration of Lord Hood at Toulon and that afterwards published by His Majesty, addressed to the people of France. These declarations, I affirm, are perfectly consistent. That of Lord Hood only promises protection to the people of Toulon, as far as he could grant it without specifying any particular form of government they chose to pledge themselves to the Constitution of 1789. The declaration of His Majesty offers protection to all the people of France, who shall approve of an hereditary monarchy.

Pitt was not quite honest here as he gave rather how he wished Hood's declaration should be interpreted, than how it was in reality. It will be remembered that the English government was not satisfied with it. The affair of Toulon remained however a favourite point of attack for Fox, and as late as March. 95 he made allusion to it.

From a military standpoint the results of the fall of Toulon were the following.

First. The moral effect of the expulsion of the combined forces of four nations from the soil of France was great.

Second. The large army employed at Toulon was now free to swell the ranks of the armies of Alpes and of the Pyrenees; the friends of royalty in the south of France had no longer a *"point d'appui"* in Toulon, and the barbarous punishment of the rebellious city could not but have its effect upon other cities with similar intentions.

Third. The occupation of Toulon by the Allies had struck a severe blow at the French navy, a very large part of which was stationed here. It was of this fact that the English most boasted and with which they consoled themselves for the forced evacuation. Of the 31 ships of line in the harbour, 11 were burnt, 4 sent away with the French seamen at the beginning of the siege (this caused a good deal of criticism in England), 3 were carried off by the English and the rest saved, thanks to the rapid advance of the Republicans on the last two days of the siege. Of the 12 frigates, 5 entered the service of the English, 1 was given to Sardinia, 3 burnt and the rest saved by the Republicans. There were 13 *corvettes* of which 7 went to England, 1 to Spain, 1 to Naples, 2 burnt and the rest saved by the Republicans.

As is seen, the English received about all the ships. They were taken to be guarded for the King of France: which meant that the English had the use of them until the Restoration, 20 years afterwards. She then made excuses for keeping those of them which were left at that time. Besides the ships, the yards and naval stores of all kinds were destroyed at Toulon; but the large guns, as well as the fortifications erected by the Allies themselves, could not be destroyed for want of time. Bonaparte rejoicing over this fact wrote on Dec. 24. "*Toulon est plus dans le cas de se défendre aujourd'hui que jamais.*"

As to the historical significance of the affair of Toulon, its fall was one of the most important successes of the Republicans which rendered the peace of Campo Formio possible; its occupation by the Allies was the occasion of England's forming a brilliant scheme of indemnification, which expressed her intentions during the War of the First Coalition. But the Siege of Toulon will be known principally as the action in which Napoleon first distinguished himself. The exact part which he played in this important event has become a question of dispute, giving rise to various opinions. After studying the question I have become convinced and hope to be able to prove that those who attribute to Napoleon a great part in the success of the Republican Army are quite right.

The grounds upon which they base their opinion may often be false however. It has frequently been said that Napoleon alone, with the eye of a genius, discovered the one vulnerable point in the outskirts of Toulon, namely the Eguillette, and by this one act decided the fate of the city. This is false. He choose, as any other well schooled officer would have done, the Eguillette as a point of attack, but he is entitled to no great credit for having done so. Again according to his own statement and to that of the Representatives, this plan corresponded practically with that sent on from Paris; and again, the Allies themselves recognized the importance of this point, and seized and fortified it before the Republicans could take advantage of it. This was due to the slowness of Carteaux.

The great merit of Bonaparte lay in the fact that he alone organized and commanded the artillery, which at all sieges and most especially at Toulon, played the important part. Bonaparte showed the greatest activity in the equipping as well as in the direction of this arm. Even many of the officers were called to Toulon by him personally. He showed excellent judgement in placing his batteries; so much so that, as has been seen, the shots from the first one erected, after Bonaparte had been but a few days at Toulon, announced to the Allies the possibility of their being forced to evacuate the place.

The notes of the Spanish Minster, of the English ambassador at Madrid, and of Hood are eloquent proofs of this. Almost up to the end the Republican Army was in a most deplorable state. The artillery was the one redeeming feature, the one arm which gave the Allies any concern. All their sallies were made in order to destroy the steadily approaching batteries. The daring and disastrous sortie in which O'Hara was captured, was rendered necessary by the opening of the fire of the *Convention*.

The great part which the artillery played in the final attack on Eguillette has been seen. The shots from the newly erected batteries were what forced the Allies to hasten their retreat on the last day, and consequently made it impossible for them to complete their work of burning the ships and yards. In fact the proofs of the great activity of the artillery stand out in vivid contrast to the inefficiency of the other branches of the army. The artillery was entirely the work of Bonaparte; he had the sole command until the arrival of Du Thiel, and the real command even then, for Du Theil was old, ailing and could not take any active part.

The council of war had approved all the batteries erected by Bonaparte, and the positions of all those erected after Du Theil's arrival had been chosen by Napoleon; and most of them already commenced. Du Theil was brave, well instructed and made a good impression on Dugommier. He recognised immediately the talent of Bonaparte as is shown by the following lines written to the Minister of war on the day of the entrance of the Republicans in Toulon. [4]

> *Je manque d'expression pour te peindre le mérite de Bonaparte; beaucoup de science, autant d'intelligence, et trop de bravour, voila une faible esquisse des vertus de ce rare officier. C'est à toi citoyen ministre de les consacrer à la Gloire de la République.*

Victor wrote in his *Memoirs*;

> *Or ces puissantes moyens* (the artillery) *étaient dirigés par Bonaparte; car le General Dutheil émerveillé de la justesse et de la superiorité de ses vues s'était complétement effacé devant lui; noble et rare abnégation! hommage magnifique qui honore à la fois celui qui le rendait et celui qui en fut l'objet.*

The Duc de Raguse wrote in his *Memoirs*;

> *Duthiel fut venu pour prendre le commandement en chef de l'Artillerie. Celui-ci vit le pouvoir en si bonnes mains et si bien exercé et les commandements avaient souvent alors des conséquences si graves qu'il laissa faire le jeune officier et ne prit aucune part à la direction du siège.*

---

4. War Archives. These lines have been frequently published.

He made the same statement as Victor, but attributed Du Thiel's action to different motives. His implying that Du Thiel feared the responsibility of the command is no doubt unjust.

General Doppet said in his *Memoirs*, written in 1797;

> *Duthiel fit avec moi la visite des batteries etablies avant mon arrivé et je vis avec aatant d'étonnement et de satisfaction que cet ancien Artilleur applaudit à toutes les mesures qu'avait prit le jeune Bonaparte.*

Many other less important proofs are found in the writings of those who took part in the siege. Carteaux's final praise of the Artillery and Dugommier's and Salicetti's special mention of Bonaparte during the siege have already been spoken of.

Barras also wrote in his *Memoirs* on the siege of Toulon, and it is principally upon his writings that those who deny the importance of Bonaparte's role, base their opinion. That Barras' *Memoires* are hostile to Napoleon is admitted by all who know them. That Barras' account of the Siege of Toulon is full of mistakes and consequently almost worthless as a source, will be seen by everybody who compares it with any trustworthy acount of the siege. And yet he tried to demonstrate that Bonaparte's role at Toulon was only secondary. It seems to me that he has really proved the contrary. Here are a few of his sentences.

> *Des sa première recontre avec moi je fut frappé de son activité. . . . je lui donnai devaut tout le monde des preuves de ma bienviellance. . . . Bientot admis à ma table il fut toujours placé à coté de rnoi. . . . Dugommier accorda de suite la plus grande confiance à celui qu'il appelait 'mon petit protègé'. Bonaparte ne tarda pas à en abuser; il prit bientot un ton absolute et décisif qui déplut au general en chef. . . . Bonaparte commandait l'artillerie provisoirement. Ce n'etait pas assez pour lui de ce commandement important, il fallait qu'il se mêlâ de tout et de tout le monde.*

These lines show that Napoleon made himself everywhere conspicuous. The hostile tone of the same may easily be attributed to Barras' prejudice, Further he continued.

> *Bonaparte donna quelques prouves de son talent militaire qui commençait à se developper; mais il n'agit que secondairement dans cette circonstance: je le répète le veritable 'preneur' de Toulon, c'est Dugommier.*

When one recalls the fact that on the 13th. *Vendémiaire* Barras placed his entire fortune in the hands of Bonaparte, and a few days later said to the Convention;

*J'attirai l'attention de la Convention nationale sur le Général Buona Parte, c'est lui, c'est à ses dispositions savantes et promptes qu'on doit la defense de cette enciente autour de laqaelle il avait distribué des postes avec beaucoup d'habilite,*(he then proposed him for *général en second de l'armée de l'interieur*).

And when one remembers that Barras was largely instrumental in procuring for Bonaparte the command of the army of Italy, one is justified in believing that his opinion of Bonaparte at this time was somewhat different from that at the time he wrote his *Memoires*. Barras' contemporary opinion of Dugommier has been preserved and differs much from that which he gave in his *Memoires*.

On Nov. 29 he wrote to the *Comité du Saint Public*:

*La situation de l'armée n'est pas satisfaisante. Je suis loin d'inculper le général Dugommier. Cependent ce général questionné par moi n'a pu me dire le nombre de troupes qu'il commande; il ignore le nom des bataillons arrivées, le nom et le nombre de ceux qu'il attend; il n'avait encore fait ni fait faire aucune revue, il ne connaissait pas la situation de ses principales batteries; je l'ai exhorté à s'occuper plus serieusement de la grande affaire dont vous l'avez chargé et de surveiller toutes les parties de l'administration qui m'ont paru très negligées; il m'a tout promis; il m'a paru très bien intentioné, puisse-t-il tenir parole.*

Barras' opinion of Dugommier may be of no great value but it seems strange to see him write in this tone of him whom he afterwards termed the "*veritable preneur de Toulon*." Further he wrote.

*La prise du Général O'Hara attribué à Bonaparte, le vaiseau qu'il aurait coulé bas, le plan de campagne auquel il aurait participé sont autont d'assertions fausses, imaginées par celui qui en a imaginé bien d'autres, répétées par ses flatteurs le jour où il a eu l'argent pour les payer.*

These lines show the style and spirit in which Barras wrote of Napoleon. The statements are quite false. It is true that Bonaparte did not personally take O'Hara prisoner, and he nowhere said that he did. It is however practically certain that he commanded the body of troops who found the wounded English General. As for the "*vaisseau Anglais*," he sank several shortly after his arrival at Toulon, as has been seen. As for the plan of attack, it has been shown how he selected it as the proper one from the very first and followed it up to the end. Barras' ideas on the proper manner of attacking Toulon I have found in a letter—written by him at that time, and as it is unpublished I have given it in full, (see Appendix 2).

Reading it one cannot but admit that it is merely a mass of phrases put together by one who feels he is bound to say something on a subject of which he knows little. It shows that Barras is not a military man: consequently his opinion of Bonaparte's participation in a plan which he himself did not appreciate, is worthless. On Nov. 29. he wrote of the plan decided upon by the council of war. . . . *"Je l'ai trouvé très bien écrit, fort bien rédigé, même assez bien concu."*

Again nothing but phrases, where Barras' criticises the handwriting and literary merit of a military plan. It must surely be admitted that to judge of Napoleon's role at the Siege of Toulon from Barras' *memoires* is quite untrustworthy, in fact worse, as they are incorrect and biased. Others [5] who have written on this event, say that nothing in the official records shows the great role played by Bonaparte. It is true that in the War Archives in Paris there is no exact statement, nor is it mathematically demonstrated that Bonaparte played the principal part in the Siege of Toulon: but indirect proofs abound even here and are also to be found in the sources of the English and of the other Allies. History is not an exact science; therefore a fact which, even through an indirect proof appeals to the reason of an unprejudiced person is taken as truth. It is quite as wrong to deny a fact which is clear, as to assert one which is false. Toulon was Bonaparte's opportunity and he took every advantage of it.

It is instructive to follow as closely as the material permits, Bonaparte's actions during these three important months: to see how during this time of jealousy, distrust and open enmity between the different officers, and between the commanding officer and Representatives, Bonaparte understood how to remain on excellent terms with them all and to continue his part of the undertaking, conscious of his aim and uninterrupted in his progress. Napoleon, spurred on by his restless ambition and armed with an excellent technical instruction, needed yet something more to forward him in his wonderful career;, to keep him on the proper path, and from wasting his untiring energy against impossibilities. He needed a broad knowledge of men and a clear insight into the conditions of his day.

Without this he might have been a Hoche, a Kleber or a Ney, but never a Napoleon nor even a Bernadotte. His intuitive genius could not of itself have supplanted such knowledge; it made him quick in comprehending, arranging and generalizing his experience, but the experience itself was necessary. Napoleon may have needed less than

5. Jung; Krebs and Morris.

others, but he needed some. Such an experience of the world of his day could not have been acquired in an artillery school in Brienne, nor in the little island of Corsica, dealing with a unique people, nor had Bonaparte obtained it as yet in France. His *Souper de Beaucaire* shows that his views and ideas were still limited. It is first at Toulon that he acquired this broader and valuable experience.

Here he took an active and important part, right in the centre of an event of European importance. He was in touch with revolutionary France, with the representatives, and generals; an interested spectator of party strife and of the conflict of political and social ideas. He came into contact with the European nations, lived in an atmosphere of uncertainty, danger and intrigue. Even from a military stand-point he must have learned a great deal. Here he witnessed the combined action of the different arms, with a preponderance of his own special one. He realized the importance of that department which provides for the provisioning of the army.

All this must have made a vivid and lasting impression on the mind of Bonaparte, then a young man, awaiting an opportunity. How well he understood human nature is demonstrated by the tact with which he won the confidence of all those with whom he came in contact, the Representatives, among them Barras; the Generals Dutheil, Doppet and Dugommier. His naming an exposed battery in which the gunners hesitated to serve, *La batterie des Hommes-sans peur*, and in this way so touching their pride that everyone strove for the honour of serving in it, shows how well he understood his soldiers. One is reminded of his address to his army in Italy two years later.

Napoleon made many friends at Toulon; among them several of his future lieutenants, Junot, Marmont, Victor and others. His relations with the younger of the Robespierres nearly dragged him down in their fall, and it was undoubtedly here that arose the enmity between Napoleon and his countryman Arena who was afterwards executed for an attempt on the life of the First Consul. But these were exceptions. It was certainly not at Toulon that he won the hatred of Barras; quite the contrary. Men as well as conditions he used to his best advantage. Yet one cannot accuse him of ingratitude.

All of those who still lived when he was in power, and the sons and grandsons of those who did not were rewarded; many of them in his will from St. Helena. It is a grand sight to see how the dethroned Emperor recalls and rewards those who helped him in his early career. All this experience, good luck and self-satisfaction was no doubt what made Napoleon feel that his history should begin with the siege of Toulon. Yet he seemed to forget that his thoughts, sentiments and actions before this period were also of great interest to those who wished to study the career of one of the world's exceptional men.

# Appendix 1

[Record Office.]

Trevor to Grenville.                                    Turin Dec. 14.

―― ―― ―― *Monsieur* is expected here the 16th and your Lordship may depend on a faithful execution of the instructions therein alluded to, the Importance of which I see in the strongest sense and the more so because suspicions I have for sometime entertained are more than ever confirmed that the Spaniards are at the bottom of a secret intrigue of placing *Monsieur* at Toulon in his character of Regent. Your Lordship heard enough of their behaviour at Toulon to conceive what suggestions and what hopes their jealousy and disappointed pride may have given birth to.

The princes of the blood have had some secret agents at Toulon and I learn from thence in a private letter of the seventh instant that His Majesty's commissaries knew nothing of *Monsieur's* journey towards that place that the Spaniards had found means to gain a party amongst the sections and that a sort of wish had been expressed by them that *Monsieur* should be called there as regent that this idea had been communicated to Sir Gilbert Elliot and that he did not seem to consider it liable to any great inconvenience.

If it is indeed true the dispositions at Toulon are such, a part of our objections would be removed but there still remains others which I shall consider as an insult, till I receive from your Lordship positive orders to the contrary; and first the surreptitious manner in which it appears to be conducted and the want of any previous application for His Majesty's permission which was equally necessary from a principle both of policy and respect and secondly the weighty consideration that it is not enough that this measure should be thought politic by the inhabitants of Toulon.

It must also be considered so by His Majesty's ministers and as consistent with those principles which constitute the wish for the support of a vigorous government.

# Appendix 2

[*Archives Nationales.*]

*Paul Barras à ses collegues à Ollioules.*

*J'ai reflechi mes chers collegues sur le plan d'attaque propose par le gé-
néral et approuvé par vous. je crois devoir vous reiterer par écrit et pour
l'interet de la Republique une partie de mes observations. Les deux
divisions de l'ouest et de l'est dirigées contre Toulon doivent attaquer
dans toute leur étendu tous les postes des ennemis, parmis ces attaques il
en est d'effective et de fausses. J'ose croire d'abord que les principales de
ces attaques doivent être diriger contre Pharon, la chartreuse l'aiguillette
ou Balaguier et Malbousquet. Deux attaques que je regarde comme
decisives et devant produire subitement la prise de Toulon si elles reuis-
sissent sont celles de Pharon et de Malbosquet.*

*Je pense donc qu'il faut surtout s'attacher plus particulairement à la pris
de ses deux positions et que les colonnes ou les differentes corps destinés
pour ces deux attaques doivent être nombreuses et bien choisis. Je pense
que les aproches doivent être faites avant le jour et le lendemain d'une
grande canonade qui aura démonté les canons de l'enemie et demoli
ses travaux.*

*Je pense qu'il doit être defendu de tirer un seul coup de fusil, qu'il faut
joindre l'ennemi et user de l'arme blanche, qu l'impetuosité francaise
rend presque toujours favorables. Je pense qu'il faut aussi prevoir tous
les cas; que le resultat des attaques les mieux conbinées est quelque fois
contrarié et qu'alors des pointes de ralliement doivent être convenues;
des lignes ou retranchements élevés pour y recevoir les troupes repoussés
ou poursuivis ainsi que des pieces de position placées dans ces retranchements.*

*Je pense qu'il faut choisir les travailleurs et preparer en abbondance
tout ce qui sera necessaire pour se loger et se retrancher aussitôt qu'on
sera maître de quelque poste ennemie. Si des postes et Pharon surtout*

109

sout pris le général doit s'attendre à de grands efforts de la parte des ennemis pour reprendre ces positions d'ou depend leur salut; il doit en consequence s'y fortifier sur le champ y caserner des troupes sures et nombreuses, en longer même sur les derrieres pour les appeller au besoin.

Pour attaquer à la fois une lingue aussi étendue que celle de la droite de la rade de Toulon à sa gauche il faut de bonnes troupes, je suis d'avis d'attaquer sans retard mais je tiens à ce que 6000 soient sur le champ détachés de l'armée d'Italie et envoyé sur Toulon alors je ne considere plus le succes de l'attaque projettée comme incertaine, alors je n'hesite plus d'assurer que les infames brigands renferés dans Toulon n'auront autre parti que la fuite et la mort qui les poursuivera.

Quelles sont les forces effectives de l'armée de la Republique sous les murs de Toulon? quelest le nombre des bataillons qui les composent? je n'ai pu avoir à cet égard qu'une donnée aproximative qui la porte à 30,000 hommes et parmi laquelle on pent compter moitie de p. requisition. Si l'ennemi a 15, 18 ou vingt mille hommes, car je n'ai encore à cet égard aucune certitude vous hasardez peutêtre en attaquant de cette manière non seulement le sort de l'armée francaise mais celui du midi; vous perdez au moins l'espoir d'entreprendre de nouvelles attaques et vous êtes obligés d'attendre les forces et l'attirall immense, mais necessaire pour faire un siège auquel l'ennemi aura tout le temps de se preparer.

Observez encore que par la distance et la nature de vos positions il est impossible qu'elles se soutienent et se protegent mutuellement. L'armée d'Italie est fermée par les neiges, le tableau que nous en a fait Dugomier est très rassurant. 6000 hommes de troupes experimentées et agueries en seroient détachées pour l'attaque de Toulon, cela nous donnerait alors une masse de force une préponderance une confiance même à nos troupes qui nous assure du succès. Ces 6000 hommes seroient remplacés à l'armée d'Italie par des bataillons de premiere requisition, ainsi nul inconvenient d'executer de suite cete mesure.

Je vous soumis de nouveau toutes ces observations peser les dans votre sagesse communiquez les au général, ne perdez pas de vue que la destruction de Toulon tient au salut du midi qu'il n'est aucun sacrifice aucune consideration qui doivent vous arrêter lorsque il est question de chasser l'ennemi de ce post important observez aussi qu'alors vous pourrez disposer d'une armée victorieuse et sauver la Republique en admettant tous les moyens que je vous ai demontré.

Au reste il faut que Toulon soit attaqué et qu'il le soit vigoureusement si mes observations sont rejettées je me rendrai à l'armée et avec nos *propres moyens nous executerons le plan proposé.*

*A Marseille le 8 frimaire l'an 2 de la Republique.*

*Paul Barras.*

LEONAUR

# ALSO FROM LEONAUR
## AVAILABLE IN SOFTCOVER OR HARDCOVER WITH DUST JACKET

**LIFE IN THE ARMY OF NORTHERN VIRGINIA** *by Carlton McCarthy*—The Observations of a Confederate Artilleryman of Cutshaw's Battalion During the American Civil War 1861-1865.

**HISTORY OF THE CAVALRY OF THE ARMY OF THE POTOMAC** *by Charles D. Rhodes*—Including Pope's Army of Virginia and the Cavalry Operations in West Virginia During the American Civil War.

**CAMP-FIRE AND COTTON-FIELD** *by Thomas W. Knox*—A New York Herald Correspondent's View of the American Civil War.

**SERGEANT STILLWELL** *by Leander Stillwell* —The Experiences of a Union Army Soldier of the 61st Illinois Infantry During the American Civil War.

**STONEWALL'S CANNONEER** *by Edward A. Moore*—Experiences with the Rockbridge Artillery, Confederate Army of Northern Virginia, During the American Civil War.

**THE SIXTH CORPS** *by George Stevens*—The Army of the Potomac, Union Army, During the American Civil War.

**THE RAILROAD RAIDERS** *by William Pittenger*—An Ohio Volunteers Recollections of the Andrews Raid to Disrupt the Confederate Railroad in Georgia During the American Civil War.

**CITIZEN SOLDIER** *by John Beatty*—An Account of the American Civil War by a Union Infantry Officer of Ohio Volunteers Who Became a Brigadier General.

**COX: PERSONAL RECOLLECTIONS OF THE CIVIL WAR--VOLUME 1** *by Jacob Dolson Cox*—West Virginia, Kanawha Valley, Gauley Bridge, Cotton Mountain, South Mountain, Antietam, the Morgan Raid & the East Tennessee Campaign.

**COX: PERSONAL RECOLLECTIONS OF THE CIVIL WAR--VOLUME 2** *by Jacob Dolson Cox*—Siege of Knoxville, East Tennessee, Atlanta Campaign, the Nashville Campaign & the North Carolina Campaign.

**KERSHAW'S BRIGADE VOLUME 1** *by D. Augustus Dickert*—Manassas, Seven Pines, Sharpsburg (Antietam), Fredricksburg, Chancellorsville, Gettysburg, Chickamauga, Chattanooga, Fort Sanders & Bean Station.

**KERSHAW'S BRIGADE VOLUME 2** *by D. Augustus Dickert*—At the wilderness, Cold Harbour, Petersburg, The Shenandoah Valley and Cedar Creek..

AVAILABLE ONLINE AT www.leonaur.com
AND FROM ALL GOOD BOOK STORES          07/09

LEONAUR

# ALSO FROM LEONAUR
## AVAILABLE IN SOFTCOVER OR HARDCOVER WITH DUST JACKET

**FARAWAY CAMPAIGN** *by F. James*—Experiences of an Indian Army Cavalry Officer in Persia & Russia During the Great War.

**REVOLT IN THE DESERT** *by T. E. Lawrence*—An account of the experiences of one remarkable British officer's war from his own perspective.

**MACHINE-GUN SQUADRON** *by A. M. G.*—The 20th Machine Gunners from British Yeomanry Regiments in the Middle East Campaign of the First World War.

**A GUNNER'S CRUSADE** *by Antony Bluett*—The Campaign in the Desert, Palestine & Syria as Experienced by the Honourable Artillery Company During the Great War .

**DESPATCH RIDER** *by W. H. L. Watson*—The Experiences of a British Army Motorcycle Despatch Rider During the Opening Battles of the Great War in Europe.

**TIGERS ALONG THE TIGRIS** *by E. J. Thompson*—The Leicestershire Regiment in Mesopotamia During the First World War.

**HEARTS & DRAGONS** *by Charles R. M. F. Crutwell*—The 4th Royal Berkshire Regiment in France and Italy During the Great War, 1914-1918.

**INFANTRY BRIGADE: 1914** *by John Ward*—The Diary of a Commander of the 15th Infantry Brigade, 5th Division, British Army, During the Retreat from Mons.

**DOING OUR 'BIT'** *by Ian Hay*—Two Classic Accounts of the Men of Kitchener's 'New Army' During the Great War including *The First 100,000 & All In It.*

**AN EYE IN THE STORM** *by Arthur Ruhl*—An American War Correspondent's Experiences of the First World War from the Western Front to Gallipoli-and Beyond.

**STAND & FALL** *by Joe Cassells*—With the Middlesex Regiment Against the Bolsheviks 1918-19.

**RIFLEMAN MACGILL'S WAR** *by Patrick MacGill*—A Soldier of the London Irish During the Great War in Europe including *The Amateur Army*, *The Red Horizon* & *The Great Push.*

**WITH THE GUNS** *by C. A. Rose & Hugh Dalton*—Two First Hand Accounts of British Gunners at War in Europe During World War 1- Three Years in France with the Guns and With the British Guns in Italy.

**THE BUSH WAR DOCTOR** *by Robert V. Dolbey*—The Experiences of a British Army Doctor During the East African Campaign of the First World War.

LEONAUR

# ALSO FROM LEONAUR
### AVAILABLE IN SOFTCOVER OR HARDCOVER WITH DUST JACKET

**THE 9TH—THE KING'S (LIVERPOOL REGIMENT) IN THE GREAT WAR 1914 - 1918** *by Enos H. G. Roberts*—Mersey to mud—war and Liverpool men.

**THE GAMBARDIER** *by Mark Severn*—The experiences of a battery of Heavy artillery on the Western Front during the First World War.

**FROM MESSINES TO THIRD YPRES** *by Thomas Floyd*—A personal account of the First World War on the Western front by a 2/5th Lancashire Fusilier.

**THE IRISH GUARDS IN THE GREAT WAR - VOLUME 1** *by Rudyard Kipling*—Edited and Compiled from Their Diaries and Papers—The First Battalion.

**THE IRISH GUARDS IN THE GREAT WAR - VOLUME 1** *by Rudyard Kipling*—Edited and Compiled from Their Diaries and Papers—The Second Battalion.

**ARMOURED CARS IN EDEN** *by K. Roosevelt*—An American President's son serving in Rolls Royce armoured cars with the British in Mesopatamia & with the American Artillery in France during the First World War.

**CHASSEUR OF 1914** *by Marcel Dupont*—Experiences of the twilight of the French Light Cavalry by a young officer during the early battles of the great war in Europe.

**TROOP HORSE & TRENCH** *by R.A. Lloyd*—The experiences of a British Life-guardsman of the household cavalry fighting on the western front during the First World War 1914-18.

**THE EAST AFRICAN MOUNTED RIFLES** *by C.J. Wilson*—Experiences of the campaign in the East African bush during the First World War.

**THE LONG PATROL** *by George Berrie*—A Novel of Light Horsemen from Gallipoli to the Palestine campaign of the First World War.

**THE FIGHTING CAMELIERS** *by Frank Reid*—The exploits of the Imperial Camel Corps in the desert and Palestine campaigns of the First World War.

**STEEL CHARIOTS IN THE DESERT** *by S. C. Rolls*—The first world war experiences of a Rolls Royce armoured car driver with the Duke of Westminster in Libya and in Arabia with T.E. Lawrence.

**WITH THE IMPERIAL CAMEL CORPS IN THE GREAT WAR** *by Geoffrey Inchbald*—The story of a serving officer with the British 2nd battalion against the Senussi and during the Palestine campaign.

www.ingramcontent.com/pod-product-compliance
Lightning Source LLC
Chambersburg PA
CBHW031902090426
42741CB00005B/600